Discovering

Jesus

through Asian eyes

leader's guide

All you need to run eight friendly and open
discussions about Jesus, life and faith in God

Discovering

Jesus

through Asian eyes

Leader's Guide

by Clive Thorne and Robin Thomson

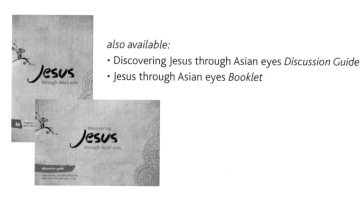

also available:
- Discovering Jesus through Asian eyes *Discussion Guide*
- Jesus through Asian eyes *Booklet*

Discovering Jesus through Asian eyes Leader's Guide
© South Asian Forum of the Evangelical Alliance 2014

www.discovering-jesus.com

Project office:
Tel (UK): 020 7520 3831
Tel: (int): +44 207 520 3831

Clive Thorne and Robin Thomson assert their right to be identified as authors of this work. SAF is grateful for the input and advice given to this project by Dr Manisha Diedrich, Sivakumar Rajagopalan, Afsar Ahmed, Matthew Irvine and Wien Fung.

Published by The Good Book Company 2014
The Good Book Company
Tel (UK): 0333 123 0880
Tel (US): 866 244 2165
Email (UK): info@thegoodbook.co.uk
Email (US): info@thegoodbook.com

Websites:
UK: www.thegoodbook.co.uk
North America: www.thegoodbook.com
Australia: www.thegoodbook.com.au
New Zealand: www.thegoodbook.co.nz

The Evangelical Alliance
176 Copenhagen Street
London N1 0ST, UK
www.eauk.org

ISBN: 9781909919198

Design by André Parker/ninefootone

Printed in the Czech Republic

Contents

introduction 7

A. Using the *Jesus through Asian eyes* booklet **11**

   1. How to use the booklet to relate to Asian friends 13

   2. 10 tips for continuing contact on a personal level 19

   3. A brief introduction to the main Asian religions 21

   4. Why these questions? 29

   5. How to prepare your church or Christian group
      to reach Asians with the booklet and course 37

   6. Organising a discussion. 41

B. The *Discovering Jesus through Asian eyes* course **47**

   Discussion 1: What is Christianity? 53

   Discussion 2: How can we relate to God? 61

   Discussion 3: How do I know that God loves me? 69

   Discussion 4: Is there life after death? 75

   Discussion 5: Who is Jesus? 83

   Discussion 6: Is Jesus the only way to reach God? 89

   Discussion 7: Is the Bible reliable? 97

   Discussion 8: What would need to change if I follow Jesus? . . 103

C. Going further **109**

   7. Leading an Asian person to Christ and follow-up 111

   8. Resources 117

Jesus through Asian eyes *Booklet*

Discovering Jesus through Asian eyes *Discussion Guide*

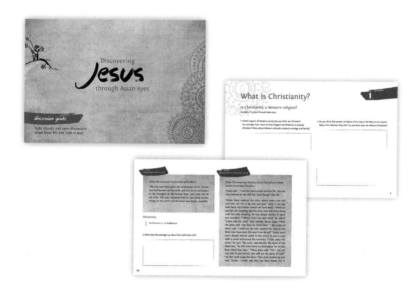

Introduction

Note: The word "Asian" can vary in its precise meaning in different parts of the world. In the *Discovering Jesus through Asian eyes* course and *Jesus through Asian eyes* booklet, the word "Asian" describes anyone from the whole continent of Asia.

Many Christians are reluctant to talk about Jesus to their Hindu, Sikh, Buddhist or Muslim neighbours, friends or work colleagues, because they are unsure of how Asians would respond or what questions they might have about Jesus or about Christianity. Actually almost all Asians are religious, and are much more interested and indeed happy to discuss different beliefs about God than the average Western person.

The *Jesus through Asian eyes* booklet and *Discovering Jesus through Asian eyes* course have been produced to give you basic and reliable resources that you can use with confidence with your Asian friends.

The booklet seeks to provide fairly brief and helpful answers to sixteen questions that Asian people from different backgrounds most frequently ask about Jesus and the Christian faith.

The course provides a biblical base from which to explore further the answers to these questions.

As you pray about starting a conversation about Jesus with an Asian friend, you can become familiar with the questions that you are most likely to be asked about Jesus and the Christian faith by first reading through the booklet yourself before giving it away. You do not have to be an expert on Asian people to use this material. This manual has been designed to equip ordinary Christians with ideas on how to use the booklet and engage in further discussion.

The four aims of the booklet are to:

1. Provide "bite-size" answers to the most common questions about Jesus and the Christian faith.
2. Clarify and deal with misconceptions about Christian belief.
3. Introduce people to the gospel message and inspire further discussion.
4. Lead on to the **Discovering Jesus** discussion course.

It can be used with friends, neighbours, colleagues, family members or other contacts in a variety of ways, for example:

1. To give away for them to read later.
2. As part of answering particular questions in one-to-one conversation or on the internet.
3. In a one-time discussion group.
4. To organise a **Discovering Jesus** discussion course.

It is very flexible. You can use sections from the booklet and from the material here as part of your conversation over a cup of coffee, or you could invite people to join you on a full structured course. You can use it with individuals or with groups, according to your situation.

It can also be used for training the whole church in how to reach Asian people with the gospel.

"It has often been hard to form discussion groups with people from traditional Asian culture as the idea does not necessarily fit with their cultural mindset, as you will read below, but I

believe that the time has now come for this to work with a new generation. There is a whole new world of Asians whose culture would be open to joining a discussion group, and this booklet can form the launch-pad for their interest to enquire further about Jesus. Without Him, the world is lost... go for it!"

Clive Thorne Minister, Southampton Lighthouse International Church

Using the *Jesus through Asian eyes* booklet

1. How to use the booklet to relate to Asian friends

Most Asian people (like most people throughout the history of the world) hold to their religious beliefs because that is what they have been brought up to do. Usually they have not reasoned out why they hold these beliefs; they simply follow the beliefs and customs of their community, although there will always be exceptions to this, especially among students and professionals. They are often, however, curious about what other religions believe.

Hindus and Sikhs believe that all religions are valid ways of reaching God, so they may be interested to find out more about the particular Christian way. Many from East Asia (eg: China or Japan), may similarly be interested. Muslims believe Christianity is the religion that preceded Islam in God's revelation to the world, and they are often keen to talk about similarities between the two faiths. Some Muslims will be eager to try to convert a Christian to Islam.

"In over 30 years of trying to reach Asian people with the gospel, including Hindus, Sikhs and Muslims, I have hardly ever come across someone who was reluctant to talk about faith. Some Muslims, Hindus and Sikhs came to a saving faith in the Lord Jesus Christ the first time that I met them, as they had

been prepared by the Holy Spirit and were seeking a real relationship with God; others took longer. One Muslim man met me every week for two years, talking about faith and trying to convert me to Islam, after which the Lord saved him! A dear Sikh friend made his first step of faith in the Lord after we had met most weeks for over 20 years ... Reaching Asian people with the gospel can be a long-term project."

Clive Thorne

Forming friendships

Forming a friendship is vital in starting to share with anyone about the gospel. Whatever the background, talking to an Asian person about Jesus is normally "as easy as falling off a log". Their culture is largely based around relationships and they are usually friendly, polite and respectful of the beliefs of others. They are also often curious to know exactly what Christians believe. The best way to use this booklet is to offer it once a friendship has been formed and an initial conversation has sparked further questions. This could lead to people joining the discussion course.

At the same time, it is important to realise that most Asian people may also have misconceptions about Christians, including the almost universal assumptions that Christianity and Western culture are really the same thing, and that we are all born into our particular religions. So we need to take time to build relationships and bridges through which we can begin to communicate beyond the stereotypes (which, of course, work both ways).

Friendships can be formed at work, school or college, or with neighbours, shopkeepers, hairdressers, etc. Food and hospitality are always good ways to begin. Be aware that Muslims do not eat pork or non-*halal* meat, and do not drink alcohol; and it is better to serve vegetarian food to Hindus and Sikhs. Accept any offer of hospitality as this will be a sign of your friendship (it will help if you like or develop a taste for Asian food!). As your relationship grows, you are very likely to receive such invitations, and this is an important part of most Asian cultures and friendships.

Similarly, learning about the appropriate history, culture and customs of your Asian friend will go a long way to building a bridge of understanding between you. A few words of the right Asian language (beware—there are many), used appropriately, will help to bring a smile and break down barriers. You do not have to be fluent but attempting a few phrases will show interest in their background.

Invitations to church social events, such as appropriate barbecues, are often accepted, especially on special occasions such as Christmas or Easter, as Asian culture especially respects "holy days". Avoid inviting conservatively clothed Asian people to summer picnics where others may be wearing very little, or Muslims to Christmas carol services with sausage rolls and mulled wine!

In Asian culture, it is acceptable for even mild acquaintances to celebrate or show their respects at major life events, such as moving to a new house, marriages, the birth of a child (a baby boy is especially celebrated) or funerals. Asian families will often invite neighbours or workmates to such occasions. By getting involved, you will strengthen whatever relationship you have with that person, and you can get to know their extended family, where you may find new friendships.

"Over the years, meeting and befriending members of extended families and their friends has been the major way of making new contacts who have eventually come to faith in Jesus. We have sometimes had over a hundred such contacts at our annual barbecue or Christmas party."

Clive Thorne

The church may have activities which attract Asian people, such as:

- mother and toddler groups
- youth groups
- English classes or other specialist classes, such as baking
- football or cricket teams, or other sports activities
- help for asylum seekers
- musical events
- lunch clubs for the elderly
- charity/thrift shops or stalls
- booktables

All of these and others represent opportunities to form friendships through social events, such as organising a Christmas party for the youth group or for those learning English.

Be a genuine friend rather than just showing interest in someone with a view to conversion. Invite people into your home wherever possible, and do not be afraid to offer to pray for them, as most Asian people would appreciate this. There needs to be trust and integrity in the relationship, and reliance on the Lord to fill you with His supernatural love.

We cannot stress this enough. Our purpose in this booklet and discussion course is to help those of us who are followers of Jesus to point Asian friends to the love of Jesus. We do that because we have experienced His love and forgiveness, and want them to do so as well. Each person has to make up their own mind about what to do after they have encountered Jesus through this material. We will continue to be their friends and to love them and serve them, whatever they choose to do.

For further suggestions and resources, see pages 39-40 (in the section *How to prepare your church to reach Asians with the booklet and course*).

Giving the booklet away

The *Jesus through Asian eyes* booklet is more than an "easy give-away" tract but less than a book, and has been designed to fill the gap for those who have just started to develop an interest in Christianity but are not ready to take on anything more substantial.

If you are offering a discussion course, it would be good to have contact details and information about the times and location of the course on the booklet when giving it away.

We should always be open to the Holy Spirit leading us in giving the booklet to friends, neighbours, relatives, work colleagues, etc. Evangelism is a work of God and so we need constantly to pray for the Lord to give us opportunities with people whose hearts are open to the gospel. In the midst of the crowd, Jesus could single out Zacchaeus in order to go and stay at his house, because Jesus knew that Zacchaeus would repent and believe in Him. Jesus remains the same today, and it is good to ask Him for discernment when giving the booklet away.

Some may have a casual conversation on a train or plane, and sense that it would be right to offer a booklet. But it would sometimes be a waste to ask someone we've just met in a shop or on the street if they would take one, as they might agree to take it out of politeness but then not read it. Asians from all kinds of background may simply believe that "God is One"; they will assume that whatever Christians believe must be fundamentally compatible with their own beliefs, and so dismiss the need to ask any questions. Some Muslims may assert the superiority of Islam and refuse to take it. It is always best to get to know the person on a friendly basis before offering the booklet. If their interest persists, you could suggest going through the discussion course.

When befriending someone from an Asian background, it is usually best to approach a person of the same sex, as traditional Asian cultures, especially Muslim ones, usually have strict rules separating men and women. This of course may be different when dealing with people who have adapted to Western ways, particularly young people born or brought up in the West.

It is worth mentioning that it is usually not a good idea to talk to Muslims in a group, as even if they are interested in what you have to say, they will often be frightened to show it in front of other Muslims. The same may apply to a lesser extent with members of other faiths, where interest in Christianity may be seen as disloyalty to their own faith.

Try to discern if your friend would be more comfortable discussing Christian faith individually or if they would be happy to join a group. Emphasise that the group will be very informal, with opportunities to express opinions, discuss and ask further questions. Assure them that the aim is to explore what the Bible says about these questions together—it won't be a religious lecture!

The group could be one that has already started, with members of your church. For further suggestions about how to start a group, see pages 37-39 (in the section *How to prepare your church to reach Asians with the booklet and course*).

2. Ten tips for continuing contact on a personal level

Once someone has shown interest, how should we continue?

1. Pray constantly and rely on the Holy Spirit to lead you in the discussion.

2. Be a genuine friend and try to demonstrate God's love: heated debate and argument are to be avoided.

3. Never attack the other person's religion as this will only alienate them. Once a friendship has been established and interest shown, areas of difference between their faith and following Jesus will become evident, but deal with them with gentleness and respect.

4. Be hospitable and accept hospitality, but remember that Muslims do not eat pork or non-*halal* meat and do not drink alcohol; and it is safer to serve vegetarian food to most people of other faiths.

5. Use the Bible respectfully: they will consider it disrespectful to a holy book to put it on the floor or on a table where there is food, or to write in it. Invite them to read the Bible for themselves, perhaps by offering them a Gospel to read. The style and content of Matthew or Luke are more helpful for Muslims, and John for Hindus, Sikhs, and Buddhists.

6. Do offer to pray for them as they will usually appreciate this. The Quran says that Jesus healed the sick and so Muslims will

often accept prayer for healing in Jesus' name. Hindus, Sikhs and Buddhists will respect Jesus as a holy religious teacher and/or an incarnation of God, and so will usually welcome prayer in His name.

7. Learn as much as you can about their background and community as part of building a bridge of friendship.

8. Share your personal story and later, if possible, introduce them to someone from their faith who came to follow Jesus; but please note that this may cause offence if done too quickly.

9. If interest is growing, offer to introduce them to a group of like-minded people from the same background who are following Jesus.

10. Be prepared to be their new family if they are rejected by their own.

3. A brief introduction to the main Asian religions

It is good to have a brief introduction to the main religious beliefs that you are likely to encounter when trying to reach Asian people with the gospel. Do bear in mind that these short summaries cover only the most basic and commonly-held beliefs of the various religions, and there exists a wide range and variety of more detailed doctrines and practice. There is no substitute for listening carefully and respectfully to your Asian friend to find out exactly what they believe and how it "works" for them. Listen carefully with a desire to learn; try not to make assumptions about what they believe before they tell you!

You can find books and other study material to help you look into these religions further in the list of other resources (see page 117).

Islam

Islam involves submitting to the authority of the word of the one and only God, Allah, as revealed to His prophets, of whom Muhammad is the last.

Islam means "submission", and a Muslim is "one who submits" to the will of Allah, who is the one God who created all things, including humanity, angels and *jinn* (spiritual creatures). Muslims primarily follow the will of Allah as revealed to Muhammad in the Quran, but also accept that Allah previously revealed the *Taurat*, or Law, to Musa (Moses); the *Zabur*, or

Psalms, to Daoud (David); and the *Injil*, or Gospel, to Isa (Jesus). Each of these revelations is seen as building on and superseding the previous ones, and history is seen as progressing towards a final Judgment. The traditions of the prophet Muhammad, the *Hadith*, are also respected and taken as guidance for godly living, although they do not have the same ultimate authority as the Quran.

Allah is seen as the same God who revealed Himself to Jews and Christians, but it is said to be blasphemy to attribute a partner to Him or to say that Isa (Jesus) is the Son of God.

The "five pillars" of Islam are: recital of the *kalima*, or creed; *namaaz*, or prayers, five times a day; *roza*, or fasting, from sunrise to sunset every day in the month of Ramadan; *zaqat*, or giving alms to the poor; and the *Haj*, or pilgrimage, to Mecca once in a lifetime.

In Islam, the duty of humankind involves obeying the laws of Allah. Each person's deeds are recorded by two angels, one recording good deeds and one recording bad deeds. On the Day of Judgment at the end of time, these deeds will be weighed up and the person consigned to Paradise or Hell accordingly. Allah, however, has the ultimate authority and can choose to exercise mercy or not. It is considered an unforgivable sin to feel sure of going to Paradise, as this decision belongs only to Allah, who controls all things.

A Muslim should acknowledge Allah's power over everything by saying "*Insha 'Allah*" ("God willing") concerning future events or plans. Muslims are called to belong to the *Ummah*, or global community of those who submit to the will of Allah, and this is seen as transcending national or ethnic identities.

Hinduism

Hinduism is a term used to describe the historical religious beliefs of the people of India.

It does not have a set creed and is sometimes described as a "parliament of religions". An individual Hindu may believe in one god, a few, many or none at all, and may view ultimate reality or God as personal or impersonal.

There are some beliefs which are common to most Hindus, as follows:

- There is one ultimate reality, or *Brahman*, manifested through count-less names, forms and images.
- There is a wide variety of forms of worship and paths to salvation. Some of these are mediated by spiritual teachers or *gurus*, and almost all ways of trying to approach God are seen as equally valid, just as "all paths up a mountain lead to its summit".
- The material world may be considered to be in some sense an illu-sion, or *maya*.
- Salvation, or *moksha*, is the release from the cycle of reincarnation, seen by some as merging back into the essence of Brahman.

Individuals are usually expected to pass through many reincarnations as they try to achieve *moksha*. They are required to conform to a right way of living, or *dharma*, in harmony with their family, caste and community. The law of *karma* (the belief that every good or bad action has consequences in this and the next life) determines the state into which they are reincarnated. The hierarchical human caste system is seen as reflecting the karmic status achieved in the previous life, the accumulation of good deeds resulting in a higher caste status in the next life. Life circumstances, such as disability, disease, success or failure, can also be seen as reflections of the *karma* of the previous life. Bad deeds can result in humans being reincarnated as animals. Hindus are usually vegetarian, reflecting this belief in the continuity of exist-ence from animal to human. All life is seen as sacred.

Sikhism

Sikhism is the teaching and way of life taught by the ten Sikh *gurus* and contained in the Sikh holy book, or Guru Granth Sahib.

Sikhs believe in one personal God, who created everything and is present within all things. He is seen as the same God of the Jews, Christians and Muslims, but He is thought to be unknowable and only revealed through His word, or *shabad*; His name/personality, or *Naam*; and through enlight-ened teachers, or *gurus*. God is not thought to assume physical form and idol worship is forbidden. Beyond this, all ways of trying to approach God that do not involve idol worship are seen as equally valid.

Sikhism is the way taught by the ten *gurus*, starting with Guru Nanak and ending with Guru Gobind Singh, and presently revealed in the holy book, or Guru Granth Sahib, which is seen as containing the spirit of the *gurus*. Sikhs should seek to remove their attachment to the things of this world and seek union with God, or *moksha*, through meditation on God's *shabad* or *Naam*.

Sikhs have similar beliefs to Hindus about *karma* and reincarnation. Individuals are usually expected to pass through many reincarnations, trying to achieve *moksha* through good deeds. *Karma* is thought to determine the state into which Sikhs are reincarnated, but they do not believe in a caste system. Sikhs are seen as being part of a brotherhood, or *Khalsa*, in which all, including men and women, are equal.

Men are given the name Singh, which means "lion", and women are given the name Kaur, which means "princess", and the use of these names aims to eliminate caste differences, which are identified through family names. Bad deeds can result in humans being reincarnated as animals, and strict Sikhs are usually vegetarian, reflecting this belief in the continuity of existence from animal to human.

Sikhs believe strongly in service to others and Sikh Temples, or *Gurdwaras*, provide free food seven days a week to feed all those who attend.

Buddhism

Buddhism is the teaching and way of life taught by the Buddha, Siddhartha Gautama, who had been brought up as a Hindu. It has no authoritative book and has developed several schools of philosophy in various parts of Asia, many of which have incorporated elements of the previous local beliefs and culture. There are big differences between these different expressions of Buddhism (see below).

Buddhism is essentially an atheist philosophy, without mention of a personal God, which sees the universe as having evolved and operating under natural and spiritual laws. The ultimate reality is seen as unknowable by our ordinary conscious mind.

Buddha is thought to have achieved spiritual enlightenment, and taught that all human suffering and evil is the result of an ignorance of the true nature of reality, which produces selfish desires. Enlightenment, or *nirva-*

na, is achieved when this ignorance is dispelled through a programme of self-perfection known as the Eight-fold Path. This involves Right Belief, Thought, Speech, Action, Means of livelihood, Exertion, Remembrance and Meditation. Buddha called this the Middle Way—between the extremes of asceticism and materialism.

People need to live through many lives to work at this self-perfection, and failure to achieve enlightenment results in continual rebirth under the law of *karma*, which reflects how the person lived in their previous life. Buddhism has emphasised non-violence and vegetarianism due to the belief in the unity of all living things. In many Buddhist countries, male monks and female nuns give up ordinary life to pursue meditation and other disciplines to try to achieve self-perfection, and often live by begging. Many give to the monks in the hope of gaining merit.

Finally, when ignorance is dispelled through the Eight-fold Path, the individual ceases to be concerned about self and earthly desires, which cause suffering, and is no longer reincarnated, but instead achieves oneness with the universe in enlightenment, or *nirvana*.

As mentioned, there are big differences between different forms of Buddhism in different cultures. For example, across East Asia (not only China) the influence of Confucianism has been strong. The recent Falun Gong movement combines traditional Chinese practices with Buddhist teaching. Japanese people follow both Buddhism and Shinto (a religion of nature spirits). Some emphasise the role of "saviours", enlightened beings who help humans, but self-reliance is also strong, as it is in Thai or Sri Lankan Buddhism (though many Thai Buddhists are also greatly influenced by spirits). Tibetan Buddhism incorporates strong belief in demons and occult powers. Western converts to Buddhism, with their different cultural background, in some ways represent yet another type.

The thread of *karma* (which leaves the ultimate responsibility to the individual) runs through them all and links south and east Asian religious traditions. Many Buddhist groups vigorously promote their beliefs.

Jainism

Jains are a small but influential religious community from India, whose distinctive focus is living with the utmost respect for all forms of life. The

Jain community today dates back to the reformer Mahavir, who lived at the same time as Buddha (about 599-527 BC).

Like Hindus, Jains believe in reincarnation and *karma* (though they view it differently) but they do not believe in gods or spiritual beings. Every living being has a soul and each soul is the architect of its own life, following the guiding principles of Right Belief (Perception), Right Knowledge and Right Conduct ("The Three Jewels"). This leads eventually to liberation or *moksha*. Jains are strict vegetarians and seek above all the principle of non-violence, or *ahimsa*.

In practice Jains associate closely with Hindus and many worship Hindu gods, alongside their distinctive Jain beliefs. Most of them work in professions or business.

Zoroastrianism

Zoroastrians are an even smaller religious community, originating in Persia, but now almost all living in India or scattered round the world. Their religion was founded by Zarathustra (Zoroaster) some time between 1500 and 600 BC. He preached monotheism and this faith became the state religion of Persia until Muslim invasions around AD 650, when some followers fled to India and settled there, becoming known as Parsis ("Persians").

Zoroastrians believe in One Creator God, Ahura Mazda (Ohrmazd), who is opposed by an evil spirit, Aura Mainyu (Ahriman). Humans must join in the cosmic struggle of good over evil and choose between right and wrong, light and darkness. Zoroastrians follow high ethical standards and are widely respected for their honesty and skills in business and other professions. They are flexible and well integrated into society around them, though also very loyal to their own community.

Atheism

There are many parts of Asia, particularly those that have experienced communist rule, where atheism has been the official doctrine for many years—China and Vietnam for example. But atheism is also on the rise in many other Asian countries, fuelled by a dissatisfaction with religion and its negative influences on life and cultural development.

But even if an Asian person you are befriending is an atheist, many of the cultural questions they will have about Christianity are the same as those dealt with in the booklet and the *Discovering Jesus* course. But they will have other questions and concerns that are not covered in the course that you will need to address separately. Atheists from Asian countries are often surprised that intelligent, modern Western people can have a vibrant and thoughtful faith in God, and this can open the door to conversations with them about the gospel.

Ancestor worship

Across Asia, respect for departed family members is a strong part of culture and religion, expressed through memorials in their honour (pictures, gravestones) or ceremonies to remember them on certain days.

East Asian cultures are strongly influenced by Confucian ideals of respect and loyalty to elders. These may be combined, to different extents, with beliefs that they continue to exist in some form, or that they have intercessory functions and can help the living, or even that they have taken on some kind of divine status.

In many homes there are pictures of dead parents or grandparents, placed in the family shrine. They will be reverenced and sometimes prayed to for help and protection. Incense may be burned, as a mark of respect or worship. Sometimes food is offered, or a feast is held in their memory, on a special day.

There is a spectrum of attitudes from simple respect to actual worship. In some countries Christians do not participate at all, while in others they take different positions: some consider such rites to be respect and veneration, not worship, while others regard that as dangerous compromise. The ancestor shrine can often be a place of syncretism or involvement with spirits. What is normally done there needs to be replaced with respect and gratitude to God for the ancestors' contribution to our lives and heritage.

Those who turn to Christ will need help in finding good alternatives to ancestor practices and wisdom to know how to take a stand graciously in their home situations.

———

If you have read this far, you will realise that there is considerable variation in every religion, as we have already said. So even if someone calls themselves a Muslim, or a Hindu or an atheist, don't assume you know what they *actually* believe and how it affects the way they live.

When you are getting to know someone, it is therefore a good idea to ask questions about their beliefs, and listen to their answers carefully and respectfully. Never attack the other person's religion, as this will only alienate them. Once a friendship has been established and an interest in Jesus has been shown, areas of difference between their faith and following Christ will become evident. Always deal with their current beliefs with gentleness and respect.

4. Why these questions?

The aim of this section is to explore the background and reasoning that lies behind each question in the booklet *Jesus through Asian eyes* and the *Discovering Jesus* course, so we can understand more about why such issues are important to Asian people. This section may be used as an aid when dealing with a single question with an individual friend, or as part of the discussion course (in which each section here is repeated).

You may already have read the booklet or at least glanced through it. It would be good to go through it again more carefully. As you read the answers to each question, turn to the notes here to understand more of the background. If you are puzzled by anything or would like to know more, it would be valuable to discuss this with other members of your church, fellowship or Christian group so that you can help each other.

1. Is Christianity a Western religion?

Most Asian people associate the Christian faith with Western society and all its failings in sexual permissiveness, drugs, alcoholism and family breakdown. They generally think that all white Western people are Christians. Muslims particularly see the "Christian" West as anti-Muslim because it attacked Muslim countries such as Iraq and Afghanistan, and supports Israel. It is wise for us to point out that Western society is not following

Christian values and principles, and that there are many more Christians in non-Western countries. We need to draw a clear distinction between what is truly and essentially Christian and what is merely Western, and remind our friends that Jesus did not live and preach in Europe but in Asia. This question may bring out issues of cultural identity, especially for younger Asians who have been born or brought up in the West.

2. Why are so many Christians not like Jesus?

Asian people are usually very religious, and if they know about the life of Jesus, they will wonder about the materialism and lack of family values that they see around them, sometimes even in the church. They may see an unfavourable contrast—between close-knit Asian extended families and looser "Christian" family units; and between the strong commitment of most Asians to follow the teachings and customs of their religion compared with the sometimes lack-lustre, half-hearted and passionless "Christianity" they may have observed in Western Christians and in those within their own culture. It will be helpful to point out that we should not judge whether or not Jesus is worth following only by the behaviour of those who call themselves Christians.

3. How can I relate to God when He seems so distant?

A personal relationship with God is not included in the teaching received by most Hindus, Sikhs, Buddhists and Muslims (though there are definite exceptions to this in some branches of these faiths); and so God may seem distant. Hindus, Sikhs and Buddhists often think that God will be unknowable until they reach an altered state of consciousness or enlightenment. Muslims usually see God as a Judge who should be respected and feared. The testimony of a follower of Jesus—of finding a relationship with God through Jesus and how it has changed their life—can be very powerful. The booklet includes a number of testimonies from a wide range of people. Asian people are almost always genuinely interested to hear of any personal experiences of God.

4. How can a good God allow evil and suffering?

This is the single most common question asked about God, and the answer seeks to take an Asian worldview into account. Hindus believe that we live in an era called *kal yug*—when evil dominates the world. They believe that people find release from this suffering by achieving unity with God through devotion, and building good *karma* through good deeds. Buddhists believe that suffering is the result of our selfish desires, caused by ignorance of the true nature of reality. Muslims believe that we should not question God's decisions but simply submit to Him and rely on His mercy. The Bible teaches that God has always wanted humans to know, love and live with Him, and enjoy a perfect life for ever—though not at the cost of allowing our sin to go unchallenged and unpunished. And it remains God's ultimate aim for His people to do away with suffering and death. God Himself suffered, when Jesus died to pay the penalty for sins on our behalf, and so He can release us from the burden of death and suffering. This idea is unique to the Christian faith.

5. Does God love me?

The idea that God personally loves us is rare in the other faiths (although it does exist in Sufi Islam and certain sects of Hinduism). Hindus, Sikhs and Buddhists usually think of God as ultimately mysterious and impersonal, and they relate more to intermediary gods and *gurus*. Muslims are often afraid of Allah and His awesome power to consign them to the fires of Hell on the Day of Judgment. The love of God in Jesus reconciling the world to Himself by dying in our place on the cross is often what opens hearts to put faith in the gospel.

6. Why does God need a sacrifice to forgive sins?

Muslims are familiar with the story of Abraham and Isaac (although they believe that it was Ishmael, not Isaac, who was offered in sacrifice). But often they are not so familiar with the idea of the sacrifices for sin in the Law of Moses, and are usually interested to hear about them. This can then lead to discussing Jesus as a sacrifice for sin. Hindus, Sikhs and Buddhists often find the concept of animal sacrifices difficult because they believe in the sacredness of all life. But there is, however, a strong historical thread of sacrifices and offerings for sin in Hinduism. Most people of any background are aware that they do not live up to their own moral standards or those of whatever religion they might follow, and so they are aware of their need for God's forgiveness.

7. What happens when we die?

This is such an important question for every thinking person. Hindus, Sikhs and Buddhists believe in the law of reincarnation; this says that people return to live many lives until they reach a state of sufficient goodness or enlightenment to escape from the cycle. Muslims believe in the "terror of the grave", in which a person is tormented for their sins until the Day of Judgment, when their life will be judged as to whether they have done enough good to enter Paradise. It is a useful approach in evangelism to ask someone what they think will happen to them when they die (in a non-threatening manner!), emphasising the perfection of God's goodness and His presence in Heaven. Almost always they will acknowledge their shortcomings and be uncertain of their final destiny. There is no assurance of getting to Heaven in the other faiths, and there is usually astonishment about Christian assurance of salvation. This then, we can say, is the reason why God sent Jesus to die for us.

8. Did Jesus really rise from the dead?

The resurrection of Jesus is at the heart of the gospel message and is unique to the Christian faith. Muslims believe that Jesus did not die on the cross but that someone else was crucified in His place. They think that Jesus was rescued by God and taken up alive into Heaven, and will return at the end of time to marry and have children. Hindus, Sikhs and Buddhists are usually much more ready to accept the miracle of the resurrection as a vindication of Jesus' message. The answer in the booklet goes through the historical accounts of His death and resurrection to highlight the evidence for what actually happened.

9. What do Christians mean by calling Jesus the "Son of God"?

This will be of particular interest to Muslims, who think that Christians believe that God had a son through Mary. Of course, they consider this idea to be blasphemous and so will often react very negatively to the phrase the "Son of God". The answer seeks to address this misunderstanding, and to reassure Muslim seekers that Christians believe in only one God, and that God did not have a son in the physical human way. This will usually lead to a positive response but raises the further question of Jesus' deity.

10. Is Jesus really God?

This question follows on from the previous one for Muslims, who are often more familiar with the idea that Jesus is called the "Son of God" than the fact that Christians believe that He is God incarnate—ie: God who became a human. It is also of interest to Hindus, who will often accept Jesus as an incarnation of God alongside many other gods; and Sikhs, who believe that all religions are revelations of the one God, who is the same for all. Hindus, Sikhs and Buddhists may not have a problem with Jesus' deity (or enlightened oneness with the universe, as some might see it). Muslims however will struggle with the idea that God could become a man, which may again seem blasphemous to them.

11. Isn't being a good person the most important thing?

All other faiths see some form of personal goodness as the way to God/Heaven/salvation. This is completely different from the gift of forgiveness and new life which comes through faith in Jesus. Buddhists try to follow the Eight-fold Path to enlightenment. Hindus and Sikhs try to accumulate good *karma* through doing good, in order to escape the cycle of reincarnation. Muslims must keep God's laws in the *Sharia* so that their good deeds outweigh their bad deeds when assessed on the Day of Judgment. However, the impossibility of being good enough for God is usually evident to someone's conscience, whatever their background. None of these faiths give any assurance of salvation or of getting to Heaven.

12. Why do Christians say that Jesus is the only way to reach God?

Hindus and Sikhs will often agree with everything about the Christian faith until it is mentioned that the Bible says that Jesus is the only way to God. Sometimes they will even agree to pray to "give their lives to Jesus" as an act of politeness to their Christian friend. But they may still believe that all religions are fundamentally the same and that this is just another way of honouring God. If this happens, they will not think they are giving up their original faith, but that they are adding Jesus as another "spiritual insurance policy". There have been many occasions when Christians have thought that Hindus and Sikhs have come to faith in Jesus, only to revisit them and find they still follow their original faiths. Hindus and Sikhs will consider it arrogant for Christians to say that God can only be reached through Jesus.

13. Can we trust the Bible?

This is a question relevant for every seeker but especially of interest to Muslims, who have been taught that the original Bible has been changed. Muslims believe that God revealed four books through His prophets: *Taurat* (Law) through *Musa* (Moses), *Zabur* (Psalms) through *Daoud* (David), *Injil* (Gospel) through *Isa* (Jesus) and Quran through Muhammad. Muslims claim that the Quran endorses the previous books, but of course there are differences in the teaching of the Bible and the Quran. Muslim scholars have therefore concluded that the original Bible must have been changed, and they will often make much of differences between translations and between the ancient manuscripts. The answer has tried briefly to deal with these doubts, and to point to the fulfilled prophecies in the Bible, which usually interest Muslims and others. Hindus and Sikhs will be much more ready to accept the Bible as a holy book, although as only one among many.

14. How should I respond if the Bible is true?

This question gives people an opportunity, towards the end of the course, to respond to the gospel message, which they have been studying. By reading out the answer in the booklet, they will receive an explanation of what it means to put faith in Jesus and why that is so important.

15. Isn't it better to follow the religion of my family?

Asian family ties are very strong and any serious interest in following Jesus will be seen as disloyalty, bringing dishonour on the family. Hindus and Sikhs may not see any point in changing religion when they believe all religions are the same. Muslims believe Islam to be the final revelation of God. In many cases, someone thinking of leaving their religious background to follow Jesus will have a very real fear of being disowned by their family. We need gently to make the point that God's truth is ultimately more important than any human relationships. The church needs to become family for those whose families reject them because of their new faith.

16. Would I have to leave my family and culture to follow Jesus?

There is often a concern among Asian seekers that following Christ would mean turning their back on their family, culture and religion by "becoming a Christian". Sadly, many families do reject members who leave their faith to follow Jesus, but it is always best for new followers of Jesus to try to maintain as much contact as possible with the family, as the opposition quite often subsides after a while. There is always more opposition for Muslims leaving Islam. Remember that under Islamic *Sharia* law, the penalty for leaving Islam is death, and such people may have to move away from their family for their own physical safety. It is, of course, possible to follow Jesus within the Asian culture and there are many Asian Christians who do. We should make every effort to help new believers to remain within their culture, and not impose on them cultural changes.

5. How to prepare your church or Christian group to reach Asians with the booklet and course

The *Jesus through Asian eyes* booklet and the *Discovering Jesus* course are great resources for the whole church to be able to reach out to Asians. Every member can:

• show friendship to Asian people.
• give the booklet in appropriate ways.
• learn more about Asians' religious beliefs and attitudes to the Christian faith.
• use the booklet in conversation and discussion in various ways.
• pray for Asian people to find faith in Jesus.
• invite them to the course.

If you are a leader in your church or a Christian group at school, college or workplace, this is a great opportunity. If you are not, approach your leaders and show them how they can use this opportunity.

You may find that there are a few Christians in different local churches who all long to reach Asian people with the gospel. It is a good idea to try to get together, to pray about contacts and the opportunities that you each have to share the faith. You will encourage one another and maybe you can share resources and work together in outreach. Any one church may have only one or two people who would really commit to prayer and outreach to Asians. But by working together, a more substantial group can reach Asians by organising outreach events like those suggested above in **Section 1: "Forming Friendships"** (p 14)—eg: barbecues, Christmas parties or discussion groups.

Here are some suggestions on how to use the booklet and course to kick-start or develop your outreach to Asians, following a simple twin-track strategy:

a) Run the course with your church or group members
b) Learn how to build your contacts and relationships with Asians

Run the course with your church or group members

Arrange this preferably with as many as possible, but it could also be a smaller group within the church/group. As you work through the discussion-course material, you will learn how to answer these commonly-asked questions and how to use Bible passages to explain the truth about Jesus and the gospel message.

This will equip your church/group members to engage Asians in friendly discussions, as well as to invite them to further sessions of the *Discovering Jesus* course. This experience will also build the confidence of your church members to invite friends along next time it is run.

"By running the course as a church, many of our members have come to understand how to answer questions from their Asian friends. Up to 12 non-Christian Asian friends came to at least one session and since then two have come to faith."

Southampton Lighthouse International Church

You can run the course:

• as a series of special sessions that you organise
• as part of your regular house groups or Bible-study groups
• as part of a Lent course or other planned series in the church
  (Follow the guidelines in the next section.)

As you run it, you can also invite Asian and other friends and seekers who may be happy to join you. They may come for only one or two sessions but that will be valuable for them and an encouragement to your members.

If you find it difficult to get commitment from church members for the complete course of eight sessions, begin by planning two or three sessions, with a definite commitment to attend. You can then decide how best to continue.

When you have run the course with your church members, you will be able to plan the best way to run further course sessions for seekers, either as individuals or in a group, as already explained.

If you would like help to start a course, for your church members or for seekers, contact the course office (see page 121). They can give you more details of the training courses and other resources mentioned below, including experienced practitioners who can guide you.

Learn how to build your relationships and contacts with Asians

As you prepare to run the course, ask how many contacts you have with Asians from other faiths. How many would you feel able to invite at this point? How Asian-friendly is your church or group?

You may already have good contacts and plenty of experience. Or you may feel you are just starting out. Or you are somewhere in between.

A range of resources is available from South Asian Concern, one of our course partners, and elsewhere, to help you build relationships, beginning from wherever you are now. These include:

- *Church audit: "How Asian-friendly is your church or group?"*
  This is a very simple tool to help your leaders assess the situation and see what further resources would be most useful.
- *Discovering Jesus: Introductory session*
  This is to help your church or group to get started on running the Discovering Jesus course. It will introduce the material, answer questions that may arise and build confidence.
- *"East+West"*
  This is a course which helps you understand the cultural and religious

background and practices of South Asians. It will take you through all the necessary steps from starting out to more advanced guidelines on communicating with people of other faiths. The course can be modified according to your situation and experience and can be run as a day course or series of shorter events.

- *On-going support*
  From experienced practitioners, as churches and groups develop their relationships with individuals and communities.

You can access these resources by contacting the course office (see details on page 121).

Some central training courses are arranged by the course office. These are an excellent opportunity to learn from experienced practitioners how best to use the course material and how to develop your ministry with Asians. For details contact the course office (see page 121).

So as you begin running the course with your church members, you should also plan time for training, as needed. As a minimum, you should include the following along with your course sessions:

- Share and pray together about the contacts that you have as individuals, and review the activities you have as a church which could attract Asian people. Pray together about how you can use the booklet and course with them.
- Form a team who will commit to the vital task of praying for the people taking booklets, and for all the existing and hoped-for contacts. Prayer is vital for this work, so it will be important to have this prayer team.
- Order some of the training material mentioned above and plan appropriate training sessions.
- Decide whether you would like to invite someone with experience of working with Asians to give advice and help answer questions. This could be particularly useful for the first session, as you begin tackling issues of culture and faith.

You don't need to be experts to begin to talk to Asian people about Jesus. But it's good to make use of resources to build up your capability.

6. Organising a discussion

As has already been pointed out, some Muslims, Hindus, Buddhists and Sikhs may be more comfortable discussing Christianity one to one because of fear of others from their community finding out.

This may mean that it will only be appropriate to go through the discussion course with one individual rather than a group. However, group discussions are also possible especially with students, professionals and young people born or brought up in the West.

Good relationships of trust and openness are fundamental to gathering Asians for a discussion. Each of the following ways is valuable, so persevere and ask the Holy Spirit to guide you constantly.

The suggestions below are guidelines based on experience. Use them to help you but feel free to develop your own patterns.

With individuals

- As part of answering particular questions in one-to-one conversation or on the internet
- In a one-time discussion
- Choosing relevant topics from the list
- In a more structured course

Using the booklet informally

1. Pray.

2. Form a friendship.

3. Give the booklet and say you would love to meet and discuss it if they are interested.

4. Meet at a café, home, in a work-break, etc.

5. Allow them to take the lead in discussing the questions they want to discuss. You could ask what they thought of the booklet, what they agreed with and disagreed with, and why. Listen first and see where the Holy Spirit leads. Ask them what further questions they might have. Try to deal with any questions or offer to look into it for the next time you meet.

6. Continue meeting to discuss in a relaxed, non-confrontational atmosphere.

7. Keep developing your friendship at other times.

With a group

- In a single discussion
- Choosing relevant topics from the list
- In a more structured discussion course

Here are some guidelines for planning a group meeting.

Timing and structure

Traditional Asian culture is very informal and often not conducive to meeting at fixed times to "do a course". Flexibility is a key component in most work among Asian people, and building relationships is very much seen as more important than time commitments or achieving certain goals in the discussion. It may well be considered rude to push for time limits or goals at the expense of personal conversation! For these reasons it will often be important not to try to force the discussion into a fixed timetable, but to "go with the flow" or "scratch where it itches" when it comes to the topics being discussed.

Traditional culture is also very polite, and often people may agree to come out of politeness but actually not turn up. They may also come along just once out of friendship or to try it out. It may be a good idea to try one session first and then suggest doing the rest of the course. Many would turn down an eight-week course but be willing to try a single meeting. If that session goes well, they may then be open to completing the course.

Many Asians will traditionally come along slightly after (and sometimes considerably after) the advertised time, and so it would be good to take this into account. It is actually considered impolite to turn up at the requested time for a meal as it is assumed that the host will be expecting you to arrive 15-30 minutes later at least!

Having said all this, students, professionals and more Western-oriented people will usually be open to the discussion course idea. In all cases, a relaxed and friendly atmosphere is best, and there should always be time to get to know each other before launching into the discussion.

A meal is an excellent way to form friendships, and hospitality is an important element in Asian culture. Vegetarian food is safest as many stricter Hindus and Sikhs are vegetarian, and it avoids the need for Muslims to question whether or not the meat is *halal*. If meat is served, remember that pork is forbidden to Muslims, and beef to Hindus and Sikhs. If you sense people are reluctant to come for a meal, suggest starting with tea, coffee and snacks. Some Asians, particularly Muslims and strict people of other faiths, do not like to eat in a house where they are not sure what meat may have been present in the kitchen, even if they are not offered it to eat.

A suggested timetable could be:

7:00pm	Leaders' prayer time.
7:30pm	Participants arrive for meal/snacks (could be advertised as 7/ 7:15pm)
8:00 / 9:15pm	Discussion group.
9:30pm	Tea/coffee and time to socialise and talk one to one.

Remember, however, that flexibility is key!

Having a meal together gives important time for getting to know one another but also enables people to come to the group straight from work. This means that the suggested timetable above could be up to an hour earlier. Dessert could be left until the period after the discussion as it provides another focus for socialising together.

Leading the discussion

On the first occasion, give specific time for each person to introduce themselves, but do not ask questions about the level of their interest in Christianity in front of the others as this could well embarrass or scare them. Be aware that women may want to sit together and may be uncomfortable sitting next to a man on a sofa.

Have enough copies of the *Jesus through Asian eyes* booklet and the discussion guide for everyone who is attending (churches may want to keep a stock for this purpose). Also have some Bibles available for reference as needed. It is very important to put these in a place of "respect"—for example, on a separate table or shelf—and never to put Bibles on the floor, or casually on chairs or where there is food. It is best if the Bibles are all the same version and are translations into fairly simple English. Some people may have English only as their second language, and different versions or long and more obscure English words may cause confusion. If some people's English is limited, it would be wise at some point early in the discussion to check if they have understood things so far, as it may be necessary to use simpler English. Try to ask a more neutral question which does not embarrass them such as: "Is the English okay for you all so far?"

Avoid jargon

In leading the discussion, try to avoid specialist Christian theological words or phrases such as "justification", "the saints", "atonement", etc as these are very unlikely to be understood. In deeper discussions, it will be necessary to define what Christians mean by "sin" (see Session 2), "repentance" and "faith" (see throughout but especially Session 7 and "Leading an Asian person to Christ"), "Heaven" and "Hell" (see Session 4), etc, as these will have different meanings in the other religions. Remember that "Christianity" is also a much misunderstood word! (See the notes on Session 1.) The discussion guide contains a dictionary feature with the Bible passages printed in it, and this can be helpful in alerting the leader to words and phrases that may be unfamiliar to participants or easily misunderstood.

State at the beginning that it is fine for people to ask questions, as people from some traditional cultures discourage questioning a host or "teacher". Never react negatively to questions or put the questioner down. If you do, it will be the last time they ask! Try to deal with questions as they arise and do not just dismiss them. Be honest if you do not know the answer, but offer to look into it for the next session.

Answering questions

React positively by saying something like: "Thank you for that thought" or "That's an interesting idea", even if a person has said something irrelevant to the topic. Be gentle in drawing the discussion back to the topic if it drifts too far off the subject. Sometimes, if subsidiary questions or topics arise that are clearly very important to the group member, it will be good to deal with them immediately. Remember that it is a discussion and not a time to preach, but always be flexible and allow the Holy Spirit to lead.

It is important to be sensitive and patient. Listen to what others have to say (even if it is nonsense) and don't cut them short. Remember that people have come from a range of other backgrounds and will have ideas and perspectives that may appear very strange to us—just as our ideas and the teaching of the Bible may appear strange to them! We do not want to dishonour a person in front of others or put pressure on people by being argumentative, but it may be necessary to move the discussion on gently if one person has started to dominate and give their own lecture.

Before finishing, it would be good to offer prayer for any requests that the participants may have, but be sensitive to the fact that members of the group may not be ready for this yet.

Always leave time for informal socialising at the end with refreshments. It may be that individuals will ask more significant questions and show more interest one to one after the group disperses, so it is important to leave adequate time for this and not to hurry away. Have some booklets outlining the gospel and a suggested prayer of commitment available to give to anyone who may be ready to consider trusting in the Lord. They will often be more comfortable taking these home to look at further for themselves, but if someone is ready to pray to give their lives to Jesus, praise God! (See the section on "Leading an Asian person to Christ" on page 111.)

After completing the course, some people may be open to continuing to meet regularly for informal chats, coffee or dinner; or may be willing to attend church or explore further about following Jesus (see Part C, "Going Further", page 109).

The *Discovering Jesus through Asian eyes* course

The *Discovering Jesus through Asian eyes* course takes people through the following eight discussion sessions:

1. What is Christianity?

Aim: To remove misconceptions about Christianity as a part of Western culture, and to show that the Christian message is for anyone from any background who truly trusts in Jesus. It is about a living, personal faith in the living Jesus, not about being part of a culture.

2. How can we relate to God?

Aim: To show that it is sin that causes our separation from God, and that evil and suffering in the world are the result of human sin, because God will not allow us to flourish in rebellion against Him.

3. How do I know that God loves me?

Aim: To show that God has shown His love for us in sending Jesus as a sacrifice for our sins, and that He wants to forgive us through this sacrifice.

4. What happens when we die?

Aim: To show that Jesus has overcome death and provided the way to Heaven and eternal life with God.

5. Who is Jesus?

Aim: To explore what is meant by the title "Son of God", and to show that Jesus is God incarnate (ie: God who became human).

6. Is Jesus the only way to God?

Aim: To show that no one can be good enough for God, and that Jesus' unique sacrifice for our sins makes Him the only way to God.

7. Can we trust the Bible?

Aim: To explore the Bible's claim that it is the word of God, to examine the supernatural prophecies about Jesus, and to give participants an opportunity to respond to the gospel. (The issue of the trustworthiness of the Bible is particularly important for Muslims and may need to be dealt with earlier in the series, possibly in the second or third session, for Muslim enquirers.)

8. What would need to change if I follow Jesus?

Aim: To show that God's claim on our lives should take priority even over our families, but that much of Asian culture can be retained when following Jesus, and we should avoid unnecessary cultural disruptions.

Each discussion session contains two topics based on the questions and answers in the *Jesus through Asian eyes* booklet. Introductory questions provoke thought on the topic, leading to further questions that are explored by reading the Bible together. The course is designed to follow a logical progression but it is fine to use a different order to deal with the questions that most affect the participants at the time. The questions for the group (printed in the discussion guide) appear in grey boxes in this leader's guide (p 53-108), and there are notes to help lead the subsequent discussions. Do not feel that you have to stick rigidly to the order laid out within each session or that you have to cover all the material. Allow the Holy Spirit to lead the discussion to what is most helpful for the participants.

As you prepare:

- Read the booklet questions and answers that relate to the topic along with the background notes in the *Leader's Guide*.
- Think of questions that may arise from the booklet.
- Read the questions in the *Leader's Guide* and think of possible answers that may come.
- Read the Bible passages and prepare any brief background explanations that may be needed.
- Make sure you are comfortable with the order and flow of the questions.
- **Important:** It will be better for you to make notes in your copy of the *Discussion Guide*, and use that in the group discussion, rather than bringing the *Leader's Guide* to the meeting.
- Pray and ask the Lord to give His guidance, wisdom and strength in leading the discussion. Remember this is not your work but His!

As you lead the group:

- Make sure that everyone has a copy of the booklet and the participants' handbook. Bibles should also be available for reference.
- Explain the subject that the group will be discussing in this session and the two topic questions that relate to it.
- Refer to the booklet question that relates to the first topic and read the answer together. You may prefer to read the answer from the booklet *after* your discussion, in order to give people the opportunity to express their own ideas first. Or you may refer to it as you go along. Decide what will work best for your group
- Only read out the notes that are highlighted! These are also printed in the *Discussion Guide*.
- **Note:** For each topic (two per discussion session), there are two introductory questions to start a general discussion. The second introductory question is optional if time is short. The next question (3 or 6) introduces the Bible passages. In the Discussion Guide it is printed after the Bible passage, but you may find it helpful to read out the question first, then have the Bible passage read, followed by discussion of the questions based on it.

- Summarise what has been learned at the end of each topic. You can use the summary, which is also printed in the *Discussion Guide*, or your own words, depending how the discussion has gone.
- If you find that time is limited, you could choose just one topic from the booklet in a session.

What is Christianity?

Aim: To remove misconceptions about Christianity as a part of Western culture, and to show that the Christian message is for anyone from any background who truly trusts in Jesus. It is about a living, personal faith in the living Jesus, not about being part of a culture.

Topic 1: Is Christianity a Western religion?

First read Question 1 and the answer in the booklet.

Most Asian people associate the Christian faith with Western society and all its failings in sexual permissiveness, drugs, alcoholism and family break-down. They generally think that all white Western people are Christians. Muslims particularly see the "Christian" West as anti-Muslim because it attacked Muslim countries such as Iraq and Afghanistan, and supports Is-rael. It is wise for us to point out that Western society is not following Christian values and principles, and that there are many more Christians in non-Western countries. We need to draw a clear distinction between what is truly and essentially Christian and what is merely Western, and remind our friends that Jesus did not live and preach in Europe but in Asia. This question may bring out issues of cultural identity, especially for younger Asians who have been born or brought up in the West.

1. Which aspects of Western society do you think are Christian? For example, how much of what happens at Christmas is actually Christian? What about Western attitudes towards marriage and family?

This highlights the truth that what happens in Western culture is not necessarily anything to do with true Christian faith and living. Specific examples of the drinking and excess that often surround Christmas, and the neglect and break-up of marriage in modern Western society, may help to stimulate thinking and get the discussion going.

2. Do you think that people can follow Christ only in the West or can anyone follow Him wherever they live? Do you know any non-Western Christians?

This questions the assumption that all Christians are from the West, and points to any non-Western Christians that participants may know. If they do not know any, you could point out some prominent examples, such as Sadhu Sundar Singh; or Bakht Singh, a very well-known preacher in India; or Mitsuo Fuchida, a Japanese aviator who led the attack on Pearl Harbor in 1941, and later became a Christian after he saw Christian forgiveness in action. It is also worth mentioning that Christianity is a global faith and that most Christians are non-Western, living in China, Africa, Latin America, Korea and South Asia, etc.

Note also that the booklet talks more about "following Jesus" or being a "follower of Jesus". You will find it helpful to use this kind of language more than "being a Christian" or "becoming a Christian" to encourage the understanding that we are not talking about becoming part of "Christianity" (= Western culture). Even though the booklet shows the distinction clearly, the underlying assumption that they are the same is **very** deep-rooted.

3. Wouldn't a message from God be for everyone?

The aim here is to show that God accepts everyone on the basis of having faith in Jesus.

Read Acts 10 v 34-43

This passage also contains a summary of the ministry of Jesus, verses 38-43, and so acts as a brief introduction to what God has done through Jesus.

a. What does this passage tell us about Jesus' life and message?

Jesus was sent by God to do good with power to heal. He was crucified but God raised Him from the dead. His disciples (His followers), including Peter who is speaking here, met with Him after His resurrection. He commanded them to preach that He will judge all mankind, and that we can receive forgiveness of sins through trusting in Him.

b. Whom does God accept? Does He have any favourites (v 34-35)?

God accepts people from every nation without favouritism.

c. Who can be forgiven (v 43)?

Everyone who believes in Jesus can be forgiven. It would be good to explain briefly about the meaning of Jesus' death and resurrection. His death was a sacrifice for the sins of the world and in His resurrection He took His place as the Lord (King) of Heaven and Earth.

Read Matthew 24 v 14

d. What is Jesus prophesying about his message?

It will reach the whole world before the end of the world on the Day of Judgment. Hindus, Sikhs and Buddhists may ask about the end of the world as this may be a novel concept for them. This is an opportunity to talk about the fact that God will one day bring an end to evil by destroying this world and bringing a new Heaven and Earth. In one of the first trials of this course, on being told of the eventual end of the world, a Hindu student immediately asked: "What must we do to be saved?"

Summary: God has no favourites but accepts and forgives everyone who puts their trust in Jesus as their Lord and Saviour. Jesus commanded His message to be preached to all mankind and prophesied that this must happen before the world ends. This means that Christianity is not just a Western religion; following Jesus is for everyone from every ethnic group.

The passage from Acts 10 gives a good summary of Jesus' ministry. It's not too soon to suggest that participants might like to find out more about Jesus by reading His life story in one of the Gospels (the style and content of Matthew and Luke are more helpful for Muslims, and John for Hindus and Sikhs) or by watching a DVD of His life. It would be good to have some Gospels and DVDs available to give away. They could also find a summary of His life and teaching at:

www.southasianconcern.org/resources/detail_2/study_packs

See the resource list on page 117 for details.

Topic 2: Why are so many Christians not like Jesus?

First read Question 2 and the answer in the booklet.

Asian people are usually very religious, and if they know about the life of Jesus, they will wonder about the materialism and lack of family values that they see around them, sometimes even in the church. They may see an unfavourable contrast—between close-knit Asian extended families and looser "Christian" family units; and between the strong commitment of most Asians to follow the teachings and customs of their religion compared with the sometimes lack-lustre, half-hearted and passionless "Christianity" they may have observed in Western Christians and in those within their own culture. It will be helpful to point out that we should not judge whether or not Jesus is worth following only by the behaviour of those who call themselves Christians.

4. Do you think it is possible that people can belong to a religion without actually following it? Why do you think this would happen?

This might help a person to question their commitment to their own religion. The second question might bring out the point that the religion of most people is simply a result of their birth. It could also provide an opportunity for people to voice any disillusionment with their religion. Try not to pre-empt these points but let people share as much as they feel comfortable with.

5. What do you think it means to follow a religion? What in your opinion is a "living faith"?

These questions are designed to provoke a discussion about the nature of real faith. The aim is to explore the difference between belonging to a religious community because we were born into it and following the faith in practice.

6. Can people be outwardly religious but not follow from the heart?

Many people in different religions like to look religious but still lie and cheat and commit all kinds of sins. Our friends may know examples of such people and so relate to this question.

Read Matthew 23 v 1-7 and 23-24

Explain that Jesus was very critical of the Jewish leaders.

a. What was wrong with the Jewish spiritual leaders?

They preached but did not put their teachings into practice.

They made many rules to follow but did not help people to do that.

They did everything for people to see, and so they liked to have a different appearance to other people with special clothes and hairstyles.

They loved honour and respect from people rather than serving God.

They liked to be called by special titles.

They outwardly followed minor laws, such as giving ten percent of their spices, but had no heart for important things, like justice, mercy and faithfulness.

b. Do you think we can be like this in any way?

This may be a question which no one offers to answer but it is included for people to think about.

Read Matthew 13 v 3-9 and 18-23

Explain that Jesus often taught in parables, which were stories of ordinary events that have a spiritual meaning.

c. What does the seed represent in the story?

The seed represents the message of God's kingdom, which Jesus was preaching.

d. What stops the "seed" from growing?

The "evil one" (the devil) snatches it away and the person does not understand it.

Fear of trouble or persecution causes the person to lose interest.

Worries and the desire for wealth distract the person from following God.

e. How do these things happen in everyday life?

The aim is to help people see what might be stopping them from seeking God.

Summary: People can be born into a religion without actually following it or having a living faith. Others can be outwardly strictly religious but inwardly unloving and unkind. Fear of trouble, worries or the distractions of worldly wealth or success can stop us from following God.

How can we relate to God?

2

Aim: To show that it is sin that causes our separation from God, and that evil and suffering in the world are the result of human sin, because God will not allow us to flourish in rebellion against Him.

Topic 3: How can I relate to God when He seems so distant?

First read Question 3 and the answer in the booklet.

A personal relationship with God is not included in the teaching received by most Hindus, Sikhs, Buddhists and Muslims (though there are definite exceptions to this in some branches of these faiths); and so God may seem distant. Hindus, Sikhs and Buddhists often think that God will be unknowable until they reach an altered state of consciousness or enlightenment. Muslims usually see God as a Judge who should be respected and feared. The testimony of a follower of Jesus—of finding a relationship with God through Jesus and how it has changed their life—can be very powerful. The booklet includes a number of testimonies from a wide range of people. Asian people are almost always genuinely interested to hear of any personal experiences of God.

1. Do you feel that God is distant from you or near to you? Why do you think this is so?

The aim is to get people thinking about what keeps us distant from God: our lack of motivation to seek God, distraction with material things around us, and our pride and sin. People may also think that God is near us because of His mercy towards us.

2. What do you think would be the result if we were able to come near to God?

The answers should give some idea of the perception people have about God, and an opportunity for you to share some personal testimony of times when you have felt close to God as you have followed Jesus.

3. What keeps us far away from God, or brings us to Him?

Following from the general discussion, this aims to focus on sin as the cause of our separation from God.

Read Isaiah 59 v 1-2

a. What separates us from God?

Our sins separate us from God. You will need to explain the meaning of "iniquities" (= sins and wickedness)—see "Dictionary" in the discussion guide. You will also need to explain what the Bible means by "sin". You may want to refer to paragraph 2 of Question 4 in *Jesus through Asian eyes* (which you will be looking at next). It deals with this and explains sin as choosing to disobey God and following selfish desires rather than living in God's love. Your friends may not have thought very seriously about sin before or consider themselves "sinful". It may be important to emphasise that sin is not just about things like murder or stealing but also about the attitude of our hearts. (See also paragraphs 2-3, Question 11, in *Jesus through Asian eyes*.)

b. What is the effect of this separation?

God does not hear our prayers and is hidden from us.

c. Is the problem ours or God's?

God is able to hear us and save us, but because of our sin He chooses not to listen to us or show us His face. So the problem is ours.

Read Matthew 7 v 7-11

This presents God's wonderful invitations to search Him out, and His promise that we will find Him if we do this.

d. Even though we have been separated from God because of our sin, what does Jesus invite us to do to come nearer to God?

Ask, seek, knock—spend time and energy to pray and seek Him.

e. How might we do this in practice?

Set aside time to pray earnestly (and maybe fast) and read His word in the Bible.

f. What does God promise if we do this?

We shall receive, find Him and His door will be opened to us because He loves us more than earthly fathers love their children. He will give us good gifts.

Summary: Our sins and evil mean that we are separated from God. But God promises to respond when we seek Him.

Topic 4: How can a good God allow evil and suffering?

First read Question 4 and the answer in the booklet.

This is the single most common question asked about God, and the answer seeks to take an Asian worldview into account. Hindus believe that we live in an era called *kal yug*—when evil dominates the world. They believe that people find release from this suffering by achieving unity with God through devotion, and building good *karma* through good deeds. Buddhists believe that suffering is the result of our selfish desires, caused by ignorance of the true nature of reality. Muslims believe that we should not question God's decisions but simply submit to Him and rely on His mercy. The Bible teaches that God has always wanted humans to know, love and live with Him, and enjoy a perfect life for ever—though not at the cost of allowing our sin to go unchallenged and unpunished. And it remains God's ultimate aim for His people to do away with suffering and death. God Himself suffered when Jesus died to pay the price for sins on our behalf, and so He can release us from the burden of death and suffering. This idea is unique to the Christian faith.

4. What do you think is the cause of most human suffering in the world today?

People's opinions may cover greed, poverty, disease, war, family breakdown, selfishness, natural disasters and more. It may be important to point out that much human suffering could be avoided if mankind shared the earth's resources more fairly, greatly reducing poverty and most disease (which is mostly due to poor living conditions and dirty water). Human selfishness is also the cause of war and family breakdown. These points turn the question around. Instead of blaming God, we are left thinking about mankind's responsibility for human suffering.

5. If God wanted to stop evil and suffering, what do you think He would have to do to stop it completely?

God would have to eliminate the cause of evil and suffering, which is human selfishness, either by removing our power to choose or by destroying all offenders. The Bible says that this is what will happen one day on the Day of Judgment. But also, God's plan is to save as many people as possible by offering forgiveness and a new life through faith in Jesus.

6. How do you think God feels about human evil and suffering?

Many people blame God for suffering but the following passages show His attitude towards it.

Read Genesis 6 v 5-6

a. What does this passage say about how God views evil?

It causes Him immense sorrow and pain.

Read John 11 v 25 and 32-44

This passage contains the same questions that we have been thinking about. The classic question about suffering lies behind the words spoken in verse 32: "Lord, if you had been here, my brother would not have died". So often we ask why God did not intervene to prevent a tragedy.

b. Why did Jesus not stop this man from dying and prevent all the suffering?

To reveal the power and glory of God (verse 40) and to show that God the Father had sent Him (verse 42).

c. How did Jesus react when He saw the people weeping and mourning (verses 32-35)?

He was deeply moved in spirit and troubled, and He started weeping Himself. God feels our pain and is not removed from it.

d. What did Jesus do in this situation (verses 41-44)?

In verse 25, Jesus says that He is "the resurrection and the life" and that He can make things right again, even reversing death. He then raises the man to life again, which is an example of how God will one day restore all goodness in a new universe.

Read Revelation 21 v 1-8

e. This passage says that God will create a new universe. What will it be like?

There will be no more death, sorrow or pain when God makes all things new. All evil will be excluded.

Summary: Humanity is responsible for most of human suffering and God feels immense sorrow and pain over it. He sorrows over the consequences of our wrongdoing and feels our pain with us. Jesus has the power to put things right and one day God will restore all goodness in a new and perfect universe.

How do I know that God loves me?

Aim: To show that God has shown His love for us in sending Jesus as a sacrifice for our sins, and that He wants to forgive us through this sacrifice.

In this session both the questions from the booklet focus on Jesus, whose death and resurrection are key to understanding and experiencing God's love. It would be good to:

- share examples of God's love and care in your own life, and in those of others that you know
- encourage your friends again to find out more about Jesus' life, death and resurrection through the resources suggested in Discussion One.

Topic 5: Does God love me?

First read Question 5 and the answer in the booklet.

The idea that God personally loves us is rare in the other faiths (although it does exist in Sufi Islam and certain sects of Hinduism). Hindus, Sikhs and Buddhists usually think of God as ultimately mysterious and impersonal, and they relate more to intermediary gods and *gurus*. Muslims are often afraid of Allah and His awesome power to consign them to the fires of Hell on the Day of Judgment. The love of God in Jesus reconciling the world to Himself by dying in our place on the cross is often what opens hearts to put faith in the gospel.

1. Think of someone that you believe loves you? What has made you believe this about them?

This explores the nature of love and how we form loving relationships. Practical actions will be seen as better proof of love than just words.

2. Do you feel that God loves you? What makes you think this?

This is designed to get people to think about their relationship with God.

3. How does God show His love for us?

Read Psalm 23

a. How is God's love for us expressed here?

He provides for us.

He restores our soul, giving us peace.

He leads us in the right way.

He guides us.

He protects us from evil.

His love and goodness remain with us all our lives and for ever.

Read John 15 v 13

b. Why is it the greatest love for someone to die for their friends?

Because they have given everything they have by giving up their life.

c. In what way is God's love completely different from any human love?

The people that Christ died for were all sinners, which means that they were His enemies. Humans will die for their loved ones, or sometimes for people they admire, but not for their enemies. That Jesus died for His enemies shows that God's love for us is even greater than the greatest acts of human love.

d. Is there any greater or clearer way that God could have expressed His love for us?

Summary: God shows His love for us in providing for us, refreshing us, leading and guiding us, and protecting us from evil all our lives. But the greatest way He has shown His love is by sending Jesus to save us from judgment by dying on the cross to pay the penalty for our sins.

Topic 6: Why does God need a sacrifice to forgive sins?

First read Question 6 and the answer in the booklet.

Muslims are familiar with the story of Abraham and Isaac (although they believe that it was Ishmael, not Isaac, who was offered in sacrifice). But often they are not so familiar with the idea of the sacrifices for sin in the Law of Moses, and are usually interested to hear about them. This can then lead to discussing Jesus as a sacrifice for sin. Hindus, Sikhs and Buddhists often find the concept of animal sacrifices difficult because they believe in the sacredness of all life. But there is, however, a strong historical thread of sacrifices and offerings for sin in Hinduism. Most people of any background are aware that they do not live up to their own moral standards or those of whatever religion they might follow, and so they are aware of their need for God's forgiveness.

> 4. People are fined or sent to prison for breaking the law. What would be the consequences of breaking God's law?

Everyone agrees on the need for punishment for justice to be done (which is accepted in all the other religions).

When we break God's laws, there is guilt (which may be experienced in our conscience) and punishment by God. Ultimately He will exclude us from enjoying life with Him for ever, by sending us to Hell.

> 5. If God did not require a penalty to be paid by the offender, would there be justice for the victims of crime or sin?

No. It is unjust to the victims of crime or sin if the offender is not punished.

> 6. What is the penalty that God has required to be paid for sin?

The aim of this question is to show that God set up a system of sacrifices for sin hundreds of years before Jesus came, in order to teach mankind that justice costs lives.

Read Leviticus 4 v 27-31

In the Law of Moses, sacrifices were required to atone (= make peace with God) for every sin.

> a. How important would a female goat be for a family living in a community where everyone grew their own food?

The sacrifice of a female goat would be a costly price for subsistence farmers because they would lose milk and meat and the means of breeding more goats.

b. Why do you think that the animal had to die? What does this tell us about the consequences of sin?

This rather gruesome process of animal sacrifice tells us that the penalty for sin costs a life. Explain that these sacrifices to provide for the forgiveness of sins were carried out by the Jewish people for hundreds of years in the temple in Jerusalem right up until the time of Jesus.

Read Hebrews 9 v 22

c. What does God require before He can forgive sins?

There needs to be the death of the sacrifice.

Read Hebrews 10 v 3-10

d. Look at verse 3. What were the animal sacrifices able to do?

They were a reminder of the sinfulness of the people. They also taught the people that there was a penalty to pay for sin. Sin cost a life; see Hebrews 9 v 22.

e. Look at verse 4. What was the problem with animal sacrifices? Why was God "not pleased" with them (v 6)?

The death of animals was not costly enough to pay the penalty for sin. The animal sacrifices were only symbols of the real sacrifice that would need to be made for sin.

Read 1 Peter 2 v 24

f. What is the real sacrifice that provides forgiveness for sins?

The death of Jesus Christ on the cross.

Summary: A penalty has to be paid for sin; otherwise there would be no justice for the victims. God required animal sacrifices as symbolic reminders to people that their sins could only be forgiven through the cost of a life. Animal sacrifices were symbolic previews of the real sacrifice for sin, which was Jesus' death on the cross.

Is there life after death?

Aim: To show that Jesus has overcome death and provided the way to Heaven and eternal life with God.

Topic 7: What happens when we die?

First read Question 7 and the answer in the booklet.

This is such an important question for every thinking person. Hindus, Sikhs and Buddhists believe in the law of reincarnation; this says that people return to live many lives until they reach a state of sufficient goodness or enlightenment to escape from the cycle. Muslims believe in the "terror of the grave", in which a person is tormented for their sins until the Day of Judgment, when their life will be judged as to whether they have done enough good to enter Paradise. It is a useful approach in evangelism to ask someone what they think will happen to them when they die (in a non-threatening manner!), emphasising the perfection of God's goodness and His presence in Heaven. Almost always they will acknowledge their shortcomings and be uncertain of their final destiny. There is no assurance of getting to Heaven in the other faiths, and there is usually astonishment about Christian assurance of salvation. This then, we can say, is the reason why God sent Jesus to die for us.

1. What do you think Heaven is like? Do you think that there will be any evil or sin there at all?

Muslims think of Heaven as a sort of earthly-style Paradise with sensual pleasures. Some Hindus, Sikhs and Buddhists believe in a merging of our individuality into the oneness of everything, while others believe in some kind of Heaven. These questions aim to encourage people to think in terms of the moral environment of Heaven.

2. Do you think that God will allow us into Heaven as we are or will we need to change? If so, how?

Almost everyone will admit that we could not go to Heaven as we are and would need to be made morally perfect.

3. Could anything impure or imperfect be allowed into Heaven?

Read Revelation 21 v 22-27

Explain that this is part of a vision of Heaven given to Jesus' disciple John, and that it is therefore set in picture language and symbolism. No one can really visualise or imagine what Heaven is like (see 1 Corinthians 2 v 9).

a. What gives the light in Heaven? What does this mean?

The glory of God is its light (verse 23), which speaks of God's purity filling Heaven.

b. Will anything impure ever enter it? What is excluded?

Nothing impure, shameful or deceitful can ever enter (verse 27).

c. Who can enter Heaven?

Only those whose names are written in the Lamb's book of life can enter Heaven (verse 27). The Lamb is a title given to Jesus, which the next Bible reading will explain.

Read John 1 v 29

Explain that "John" is John the Baptist, the prophet who came to prepare the way for Jesus. In this verse he points out who Jesus is and what He has come to do.

d. Who is the Lamb (the one who was sacrificed to take away the sin of the world)?

Jesus is the Lamb of God. He became the sacrifice that was needed to pay the penalty for our sin so that we can be accepted by God into Heaven.

e. What does it mean to be in the Lamb's book of life (Revelation 21 v 27)?

We are in Jesus' book of life if we are given forgiveness and eternal life by Him.

Summary: Heaven is a perfect place where no evil can be allowed to enter, and so our sins have to be forgiven and we have to be made new in order to go there. This forgiveness and new life come through putting our trust in Jesus Christ as our Lord and Saviour.

How do we know all this is true? Only Jesus has come back from death to tell us this, and so we need to look carefully at the Bible's account of His resurrection.

Topic 8: Did Jesus really rise from the dead?

First read Question 8 and the answer in the booklet.

The resurrection of Jesus is at the heart of the gospel message and is of course unique to the Christian faith. Muslims believe that Jesus did not die on the cross but that someone else was crucified in His place. They think that Jesus was rescued by God and taken up alive into Heaven, and will return at the end of time to marry and have children. Hindus, Sikhs and Buddhists are usually much more ready to accept the miracle of the resurrection as a vindication of Jesus' message. The answer in the booklet goes through the historical accounts of His death and resurrection to highlight the evidence for what actually happened.

> 4. If you were one of the disciples, what might you have felt when Jesus was arrested, tried and executed?

This gets people to imagine the disciples' reaction when they saw Jesus' ministry ended by His arrest and execution.

> 5. Do you think that anyone seriously expected Jesus to come back from the dead?

This brings out the point that people in the first century were no more likely than we are to expect someone to rise from the dead, so something must have happened to transform the disciples.

> 6. What did the disciples say about Jesus' resurrection?

This section examines some of the firsthand accounts of the resurrection.

Read Acts 2 v 22-36

This is part of the first ever Christian message preached by Jesus' apostle, Peter, near the temple in Jerusalem about seven weeks after the resurrection (Jesus had appeared alive over a period of 40 days). Peter emphasises the fact that Jesus rose from the dead, so He wasn't just a prophet and a good man, and so we should all follow His teaching.

a. What are the main points that Peter wants to communicate?

Jesus has been raised from the dead.

This was predicted by the prophet David (Psalms 16 v 8-11 and 110 v 1) about 1,000 years before Jesus was born.

Peter and the other disciples are all witnesses of the resurrection.

b. Peter quotes, in verses 25-28, a psalm written by King David about 1,000 years before Jesus. How does he show that this predicts Jesus' resurrection?

David clearly died (verse 29) but he says that the "holy one" will not see decay (verse 27). David could not have been speaking about himself, but about someone in the future.

c. Peter quotes another psalm of David in verses 34-35. How does David's psalm, as explained by Peter, show that Jesus is Lord over creation?

David was buried (verse 29) and clearly did not ascend into Heaven (verse 34), but his descendant, Jesus, did ascend to Heaven to take up His role as Lord and King over humanity. This happened 40 days after Jesus' resurrection, and was seen by His disciples.

Read 1 Corinthians 15 v 3-20

This is Paul's summary of several of Jesus' resurrection appearances, written around AD 54, just 20 years after the events. It describes the message that the apostles had been preaching for all those years.

d. Why do you think Paul describes Jesus' resurrection appearances as being at the heart of the message about Jesus?

The resurrection confirmed the truth of Jesus' claims to be the Messiah, the Saviour King promised by God in the Old Testament.

Jesus' resurrection also showed that His sacrifice for the sins of the world was completed.

Without the resurrection, the disciples would have been a defeated group without any good news to preach. Victory over sin and death was the good news of the message about Jesus. It was consistently preached by the apostles (verses 11 and 12).

e. Paul says that most of those to whom Jesus appeared after His resurrection were still alive. What could his first readers do?

The eyewitnesses of the resurrection were mostly still alive when this New Testament letter was written, so the readers could go and ask them about their experience.

f. Does the Christian message still work if the resurrection never happened?

No. Paul says that Christian faith and preaching would be useless and there would be no sacrifice or forgiveness of sins without the resurrection (verses 14 and 17).

Summary: The disciples were not expecting Jesus to rise from the dead, but afterwards they believed it had really happened. Their consistent message was that they had met with Him alive after His death. Jesus' resurrection formed the heart of the message about Jesus because it confirmed Jesus' claims to be the Messiah, the Saviour King promised by God in the Old Testament. Jesus' resurrection also showed that His sacrifice on the cross had paid the penalty for sin and had overcome death. Jesus is alive today and present with His followers to guide and protect them, and answer their prayers. He can open the way to God for all people.

Who is Jesus?

Aim: To explore what is meant by the title "Son of God", and to show that Jesus is God incarnate (ie: God who became human).

This session again presents an ideal opportunity to suggest that participants might like to find out more about Jesus by reading His life story in one of the Gospels (the style and content of Matthew and Luke being more helpful for Muslims, and John for Hindus and Sikhs) or watching a DVD of his life. They could also find a summary of his life and teaching at: www.southasianconcern.org/resources/detail_2/study_packs

Topic 9: What do Christians mean by calling Jesus the "Son of God"?

First read Question 9 and the answer in the booklet.

This will be of particular interest to Muslims, who think that Christians believe that God had a son through Mary. Of course, they consider this idea to be blasphemous and so will often react very negatively to the phrase "the Son of God". The answer seeks to address this misunderstanding, and to reassure Muslim seekers that Christians believe in only one God, and that God did not have a son in the physical human way. This will usually lead to a positive response but raises the further question of Jesus' deity.

1. Jesus is the only person ever to be born without a biological human father. Why do you think God did this?

This could lead to a discussion about Jesus' unique status among humans, since He is the only person born without a biological father. It sets Him apart from everyone else and implies that He has a different nature. (For example, He is not subject to original sin—the sin that all other humans have in them, which has been passed down from the first man, Adam.)

2. Have you ever used an expression: "Son of ..."? What did you mean by it?

You might get some interesting answers, as most examples of this phrase appear to be insulting! The point of this question is to illustrate that the phrase "son of..." usually means "like" or "representative of ".

3. What does the Bible teach about the meaning of the title "Son of God"?

Let's see what God's messenger said about His birth and the title "Son of God".

Read Luke 1 v 26-38

a. Why is Jesus to be called the "Son of God"?

Mary was a virgin, and so no man would be Jesus' biological father. Instead, the baby would be born by the power of God's Spirit (verse 35). He would be the promised Messiah, the Saviour King, who will reign for ever (verses 32-33).

b. It isn't naturally possible for a baby to be born without a biological human father. So what sign did God give Mary to show that His promise would come true?

Her elderly, infertile relative was already pregnant, showing that nothing is impossible for God (verses 36 and 37). This deals with the mostly Muslim objection that it would not be possible for God to become a man in Jesus.

Read John 10 v 30-38

This passage shows that the Jews had the same objections as Muslims have now, and so confirms that this was the original claim that Jesus was making; it wasn't added later.

c. Why did the Jews become angry enough to prepare to stone Jesus?

They considered His claim to be God's Son as blasphemous (verses 33 and 36), because it implies equality with God.

d. What is Jesus saying about His relationship with the Father by calling Himself God's Son? (See verses 30, 36 and 38.)

He is one with God the Father (verses 30 and 38).

He was sent by God (verse 36).

Summary: Jesus is called the "Son of God" because He was born through the power of God and had no biological human father. He shares God's nature and is equal with God. He was sent by God and is one with Him.

Topic 10: Is Jesus really God?

First read Question 10 and the answer in the booklet.

This question follows on from the previous one for Muslims, who are often more familiar with the idea that Jesus is called the "Son of God" than the fact that Christians believe that He is God incarnate—ie: God who became a human. It is also of interest to Hindus, who will often accept Jesus as an incarnation of God alongside many other gods; and Sikhs, who believe that all religions are revelations of the one God, who is the same for all. Hindus, Sikhs and Buddhists may not have a problem with Jesus' deity (or enlightened oneness with the universe, as some might see it). Muslims however will struggle with the idea that God could become a man, which may again seem blasphemous to them.

4. Do you think that there is any limit to what God can do? What could stop God taking human form if He wanted to?

This is trying to neutralise the objection that it would be impossible for God to take on human form, which is particularly relevant for Muslims.

5. If God did take human form, what do you think that man would be like?

Such a man would live a perfect life and would have power over all of nature. This question might be more suitable for Hindus, Sikhs and Buddhists to consider.

6. How does Jesus identify Himself?

It is often said that Jesus never directly claimed to be God, so this question aims to examine what He did say about who He was. He progressively revealed the fact that He was God to His disciples, and they did not fully realise the complete truth until He rose from the dead.

This is the night before Jesus is going to die on the cross and He starts to tell His disciples more clearly who He is. In verse 8, Philip asks to be shown God.

a. What does Jesus' reply say about His relationship with God the Father?

Jesus says that anyone who has seen Him has seen God the Father because He is in the Father and the Father is in Him.

b. Why does He say we should believe Him?

We should believe Him because of the miracles He has done (verse 11), and also because of His character (notice how he challenges Philip: "Don't you know me?" in verse 9).

Read John 20 v 24-29

Thomas had not been with the other disciples when Jesus appeared to them on Easter Sunday. He refused to believe their account of the resurrection but when Jesus appeared the following Sunday and invited him to put his fingers in the nail marks and his hand in His side, Thomas proclaimed Him for the first time to be Lord and God.

c. How does Jesus react when Thomas addresses Him as God?

He accepts Thomas' worship.

Compare the following two Bible passages:

(1) Revelation 19 v 9-10

(2) Acts 14 v 11-15

d. How is the reaction of the angel/men different from Jesus' reaction when someone tries to worship them?

They immediately correct the people, telling them to worship only God.

e. What does this show us about Jesus?

Summary: God is all-powerful and so nothing can stop Him taking human form if He wants to. We would expect such a man to live a perfect life and to have power over all nature. Jesus did these things and also clearly claimed to be God, by forgiving sins and accepting honour as God.

Is Jesus the only way to reach God?

Aim: To show that no one can be good enough for God, and that Jesus' unique sacrifice for our sins makes Him the only way to God.

Topic 11: Isn't being a good person the most important thing?

First read Question 11 and the answer in the booklet.

All other faiths see some form of personal goodness as the way to God/Heaven/salvation. This is completely different from the gift of forgiveness and new life which comes through faith in Jesus. Buddhists try to follow the Eight-fold Path to enlightenment. Hindus and Sikhs try to accumulate good *karma* through doing good, in order to escape the cycle of reincarnation. Muslims must keep God's laws in the *Sharia* so that their good deeds outweigh their bad deeds when assessed on the Day of Judgment. However, the impossibility of being good enough for God is usually evident to someone's conscience, whatever their background. None of these faiths give any assurance of salvation or of getting to Heaven.

1. No one teaches their children to be selfish, greedy or naughty, so where do these urges come from? If such evil is in our human nature, how can we expect to change into those who do good?

This is aimed at getting people to realise that sin is not just something we do now and then, but rather, that we are sinners by nature. Little children are automatically selfish and greedy because we are all born with these instincts, as part of an evil nature.

2. Have you ever met a person who could correctly claim never to do, think or feel anything wrong? In the depths of your heart, do you think that you are good enough for God?

These questions should bring out the reality that we all know we are not good enough for God. If people only think in terms of not having done major sins such as theft, murder or adultery, ask them if they think that envy, hatred and lustful thoughts are wrong also.

3. Who would be good enough for God?

Read Matthew 5 v 38-48

a. How does Jesus command His followers to treat their enemies?

Jesus commands His followers to:

- love their enemies.
- let their enemies hit them more than once.
- not only let someone take their goods but give them something else as well.
- pray for those who persecute them.

This was said at a time when Israel was under occupation by the Roman Empire, which exacted high taxes to support their army, and took slaves from the people. The command to go one mile in verse 41 refers to a Roman law that allowed the army to force a Jewish man to carry their baggage for one mile. Jesus says that if this happens, go two!

Jesus also commands His followers to be perfect.

b. How many of us would do these things? How can we try to do them?

This may be a question for people to think about rather than discuss.

Read Romans 3 v 10-24

c. Does God consider that anyone is good enough according to His laws?

God very clearly says that no one is good enough and that everyone has sinned.

d. When we understand God's laws and standards, what does it make us realise?

The more we understand God's laws and standards, as we have seen in the passages we have already looked at, the more we will become conscious of our own wrongdoing and failure to live up to those standards (verse 20). No one considers it wrong not to love their enemies until hearing what Jesus teaches!

e. What then is the way that God has made for us to be righteous and acceptable to Him?

Jesus Christ died for our sins to provide forgiveness and a perfect right-eousness from God as a gift (verses 21 and 24).

f. How do we receive this?

We need to put our trust in Jesus Christ as our Saviour and Lord (verse 22) by asking for His forgiveness and giving Him control over our lives; then we are forgiven and counted good enough to enter Heaven.

Summary: No one achieves God's standards in fulfilling His laws, so it is impossible for human beings to enter Heaven through their own efforts. God has provided the way for us to be forgiven through Jesus Christ dying to pay the penalty for our sins. We can receive this forgiveness and right-eousness from God by putting our trust in Jesus.

Topic 12: Why do Christians say that Jesus is the only way to reach God?

First read Question 12 and the answer in the booklet.

Hindus and Sikhs will often agree with everything about the Christian faith until it is mentioned that the Bible says that Jesus is the only way to God. Sometimes they will even agree to pray to "give their lives to Jesus" as an act of politeness to their Christian friend. But they may still believe that all religions are fundamentally the same and that this is just another way of honouring God. If this happens, they will not think they are giving up their original faith, but that they are adding Jesus as another "spiritual insurance policy". There have been many occasions when Christians have thought that Hindus and Sikhs have come to faith in Jesus, only to revisit them and find they still follow their original faiths. Hindus and Sikhs will consider it arrogant for Christians to say that God can only be reached through Jesus.

4. In order to answer this question, we need to remember what we have just learned about the problem we face as human beings. What is it that prevents us from coming to God? Can we reach God by our own efforts?

This reminds people of our need for a Saviour to rescue us from the penalty and power of sin. You could refer to other sessions in the course that have dealt with this.

5. The Bible says that Jesus took the punishment for our sins. Can you think of anyone else who has done anything like this?

There have been many martyrs for various causes who have died to help others, but Jesus was unique in suffering the punishment for the sins of the world. Sikhs particularly may mention that some of their ten *gurus* died to defend their faith and community. You can agree that they suffered and made great sacrifices, but respectfully point out that none of the Sikh *gurus* claimed to suffer the penalty for the sins of the world or rose again from the dead.

6. Why did Jesus say that He is the only way to God? Could there be an alternative?

This is to show that Jesus is not being arrogant in claiming to have a monopoly of truth because it is a fact that Jesus is the only one who can save us from our sins.

Read Matthew 26 v 38-39

Explain that this is when Jesus went to pray in the Garden of Gethsemane on the night before He would be crucified.

a. What was Jesus asking here?

To avoid the time of suffering that He was facing, if there were any other possible way for people to be saved from sin.

If there were another way to God—for example, if people could reach Heaven through being good—then Jesus would not have had to die and indeed would have died for nothing (see Galatians 2 v 21).

Read Acts 4 v 10-12

Explain that here the apostles are preaching after Jesus rose from the dead, and a man has just been healed in the name of Jesus Christ.

c. Is there anyone else who can save mankind?

No. Only Jesus Christ can save mankind from our sins. There is no other name of anyone else who can save us. Jesus' name in His original language, "Yeshua", means "God saves"; while "Messiah", which we translate from the Greek form "Christ", means "God's anointed King".

Summary: Jesus lived a unique life from His birth to His resurrection. He is the only way that mankind can be forgiven and find the way to God because His death is the only sacrifice for our sins.

Extra notes: Is Jesus the only way to God?

If Jesus is the only way to God, the implication that other religions are either wrong, mistaken or at least inadequate to reach God cannot be avoided. We should try to avoid antagonistic argument about this but the participants may address the issue themselves.

The best approach to this is to keep pointing back to our need of God's forgiveness, which He has provided through the sacrifice of Jesus. You could remind people of the discussion on Acts 10 v 34-35 in Discussion One, which showed that God accepts people from every nation without favour-itism. We must come to God humbly, on His terms, whatever background we are from. This is not to avoid the issue of truth but to approach it in a way that does not say: "I am right and you are wrong", but puts us all on the same level, needing to come to God in humility.

People may insist, however, that you say something about how their religion could be wrong or mistaken. One way to respond is to point out gently that teachings that contradict each other cannot come from the same source or be simultaneously true. If they want examples, you could mention that:

- some believe that sin is our rebellion against a personal God, while others deny that we are sinners at all.
- some believe that God could never become human, while others believe that He did.
- some believe we must reach God by our own efforts, while others say that we cannot.
- some worship images, while others reject that.

No one argues that all scientific theories are true; or that since all politicians are hopefully aiming for the good of the country, it does not matter which way we vote. So why should we believe that all religious teaching is necessarily true? Even those who believe there are many ways to God (for example Hindus) do not say that ALL beliefs are true. Would we accept every religion as valid when some religions, such as that of the Mayans and Aztecs of Central America, advocated human sacrifice?

A related question may arise about what happens to those who do not hear about Jesus. It would be good to look at Romans 1 v 20 and 2 v 12-16. God says that all mankind knows that there is a God and has a conscience about what is right and wrong, informing them when they do wrong. Given that everyone will be condemned by their own conscience, God expects all people to seek His forgiveness, and does not judge people on what they do not know (see Acts 17 v 26-31). All those who seek will find (Matthew 7 v 7-8). It would be good to give examples of those who knew nothing about Jesus Christ, but who sought God and received visions, dreams and messages from God telling them about Jesus, such as Cornelius in Acts 10 v 1-6.

If our Asian friend of whatever other faith is eventually to come to follow Jesus, they would need to accept that they are leaving their previous religious allegiance. This discussion session (especially if it is in a group) is not necessarily the best time to address this point, but they may want to ask about it themselves. This will be dealt with very specifically in Discussion Eight (Questions 15 and 16 in the booklet). It would be good for you to read that material as you prepare for this session.

The above points may be helpful if discussed in an atmosphere of gentleness and respect but it may be best to try to talk about these issues later one to one.

Is the Bible reliable?

Aim: To explore the Bible's claim that it is the word of God, to examine the supernatural prophecies about Jesus, and to give participants an opportunity to respond to the gospel. (The issue of the trustworthiness of the Bible is particularly important for Muslims and may need to be dealt with earlier in the series, possibly in the second or third session, for Muslim enquirers.)

Topic 13: Can we trust the Bible?

First read Question 13 and the answer in the booklet.

This is a question relevant for every seeker but especially of interest to Muslims, who have been taught that the original Bible has been changed. Muslims believe that God revealed four books through His prophets: *Taurat* (Law), *Zabur* (Psalms), *Injil* (Gospel) and *Quran*. Muslims claim that the Quran endorses the previous books, but of course there are differences in the teaching of the Bible and the Quran. Muslim scholars have therefore concluded that the original Bible must have been changed, and they will often make much of differences between translations and between the ancient manuscripts.

The answer has tried briefly to deal with these doubts, and to point to the fulfilled prophecies in the Bible, which usually interest Muslims and others. Hindus and Sikhs will be much more ready to accept the Bible as a holy book, although as only one among many.

1. Have you read any of the Bible before? What did you think of it? Has it influenced your life at all?

This will give you an idea about how much people have read and understood of the Bible, and an indication of where they stand in their attitude towards it.

2. Did you know that there are two parts to the Bible? The Jewish part or Old Testament (which dates from about 1400-400 BC) and the message of Jesus or New Testament (which dates from about AD 48-96)?

This will be of particular interest to Muslims, who are taught that God sent previous books before the Quran. It will introduce the difference between the Jewish and Christian parts of the Bible. The time span between the Old and New Testaments and the fact that the Jews do not believe in Jesus make the prophecies concerning Him in the Old Testament even more impressive. It may be useful to explain a bit more about the contents of the various books and sections of the Bible if there is interest at this point.

Do you have any questions about the Bible?

3. What does the Bible say about itself?

The aim of this question is to bring out the Bible's claim to be the word of God.

a. What does Peter claim for the Bible?

He and the other followers of Jesus actually saw the amazing events of Jesus' life (v 16).

They recorded them in the books of the New Testament. And what they saw and wrote was confirmation and fulfilment of the word of God spoken through the Old Testament prophets (v 19). This is completely reliable because it did not come through human interpretation but from God's inspiration. Men were carried along by the Holy Spirit of God. In the Bible, the Spirit of God is symbolised by the wind, and the idea here is similar to a ship being carried along by the wind.

Read Mark 13 v 31

To answer Muslims, who often claim that the Bible has been changed, this verse shows that God has said that He would protect His word and keep it unchanged beyond the end of the world.

b. How certain is it that God's words cannot pass away or be changed?

It is easier for the universe to pass away than for God's words to be lost.

Let us look at one of the most famous prophecies in the Old Testament.

Read Psalm 22 v 1-2, 6-8, 12-18, 27-31

The aim is to show an impressive prophecy of the death of Jesus.

Psalm 22 was written by King David in around 1000 BC.

c. What prophecies about Jesus can you see in Psalm 22?

Get people to look at the following verses from Psalm 22 and to compare them with Jesus' crucifixion as described in Matthew 27 (the relevant verses from Matthew 27 are printed in the discussion guide).

- Verse 1 (compare Matthew 27 v 46) These words refer to Jesus being cut off from God as He suffered the penalty for the sin of the world.
- Verses 7 and 8 (compare Matthew 27 v 43) refer to being mocked and insulted, using the very words that the Jewish religious leaders would use a thousand years later.
- Verses 14, 15 and 16 (compare with what happens to someone who is crucified) describe the physical suffering of hanging on the cross, with bones being pulled out of joint, dehydration and thirst, and the nails in hands and feet.
- Verse 18 (compare Matthew 27 v 35) mentions that the soldiers would cast lots for His clothes,.
- Verses 27-31 say that all the earth will remember this event and turn to God because of it, and that future generations will serve Him.

If there is time and it is appropriate, you could also look at Isaiah 53 and Isaiah 9 v 1-7 (neither are printed in the booklet).

It would be good to make the point of how impressive such prophecies are as they were written centuries before the events which they describe in detail. If these prophecies have come true, then the implication is that all the prophecies in the Bible are also true—about the Day of Judgment, the end of the world, and the need to trust Jesus to be saved from these things.

Summary: The Bible claims to be God's word in both Old and New Testaments, and it contains impressive prophecies, which came true in detail centuries after they were written. It is a supernatural, God-given book, which needs to be taken seriously in all it says.

Topic 14: How should I respond if the Bible is true?

First read Question 14 and the answer in the booklet.

This question gives people an opportunity, towards the end of the course, to respond to the gospel message, which they have been studying. By reading out the answer in the booklet, they will receive an explanation of what it means to put faith in Jesus and why that is so important.

It might be best to avoid discussion at this point and just let people think about their response. If it is appropriate, then the following questions could be used in further discussion.

4. What might stop someone from putting their faith in Jesus?

This question could make seekers think about why they may be hesitating about becoming a follower of Jesus Christ. Possible answers might include: they don't believe His message; they don't trust the Bible; they don't want to stop doing things they know are wrong; they don't want to be disloyal to their own religion and community; or, the cost of following Jesus—for instance, in losing their family and community—would be too high.

5. What might make someone put their faith in Jesus?

This question comes from the opposite angle and may provide someone with the final incentive to make the commitment to follow the Lord. Possible answers might include: they know they have done wrong and want God's forgiveness; they want to avoid Hell and to go to Heaven; or, God's love in Jesus is so good that they want to know and follow Him.

6. How can we change?

Read Ephesians 2 v 3

This passage introduces the fact that we are sinners by nature.

a. What is the root cause of our sinful behaviour?

The desires of our sinful nature lead to sinful acts. If people doubt that we are born sinful, it may be helpful to point out that no one teaches their children how to be naughty, selfish or angry, or how to lie. Children do these things automatically because it is in our human nature to be like this. This means that we are by nature cut off from God and under His anger. Muslims believe that children are born good but usually do not dispute that they do not need to be taught to do bad things (especially if they have their own children!).

b. If our very nature is sinful, how can we ever change?

We need to be given a new nature (to be born again).

Read John 3 v 16-18

c. How do we receive eternal life through Jesus?

We must put our faith in Jesus to receive eternal life.

d. Why are those who don't put faith in Jesus condemned?

They are condemned because they have not accepted Jesus' sacrifice. This would be a good point to explain that saving faith is not about intellectual agreement or belief, but about putting our trust in Jesus for Him to direct our lives as Lord and Saviour.

Summary: We should respond to God's love in sending Jesus to die for our sins by asking for His forgiveness, and entrusting ourselves to Jesus as our Saviour and as the Lord and Master of our lives.

What would need to change if I follow Jesus?

Aim: To show that God's claim on our lives should take priority even over our families, but that much of Asian culture can be retained when following Jesus, and we should avoid unnecessary cultural disruptions.

Topic 15: Isn't it better to follow the religion of my family?

First read Question 15 and the answer in the booklet.

Asian family ties are very strong and any serious interest in following Jesus will be seen as disloyalty, bringing dishonour on the family. Hindus and Sikhs may not see any point in changing religion when they believe all religions are the same. Muslims believe Islam to be the final revelation of God. In many cases, someone thinking of leaving their religious background to follow Jesus will have a very real fear of being disowned by their family. We need gently to make the point that God's truth is ultimately more important than any human relationships. The church needs to become family for those whose families reject them because of their new faith.

1. Why is a change of religion so controversial?

This seeks to explore the root of controversy over religious conversion, which is often seen as dishonouring and betraying the family and community.

In addition to the general close connection between religion and culture that we have discussed earlier, there are also legal and social boundaries between religious communities in most South Asian countries, particularly in India. The word for "conversion" in several Indian languages means "change of religion". It does not refer to inner spiritual change, but a change of community.

2. Following Jesus is often seen as a change of religious community but it is actually a change of heart. Is it good for a person to seek God sincerely and want to find God's way for themselves?

We can remind people that we are not talking about changing community, culture or family but seeking God through the way that He has provided in Jesus. Some will say that they think it is wrong for a person to seek God themselves rather than trust their parents and community, but at least this question will open up the idea for discussion.

3. Should seeking God take priority over family ties?

Since God is the ultimate Power and the Creator of all things, His claims on us must come higher than those of our family (even though those claims can be legitimate and good).

Read Matthew 10 v 37

a. Why do you think Jesus says that we should love Him more than our parents or children?

No one is greater than God and our families actually also belong to Him.

Families cannot save us or take us to Heaven.

All human beings are sinful and will make imperfect decisions and demands, whereas God's ways are perfect.

God created us and gave us all good things. Above all, He gave Jesus, who loved us so much that He was willing to suffer on our behalf, dying on the cross to save us from our sins. Such love is greater than any human love and demands a greater response.

Read Matthew 12 v 46-50

b. What do you think Jesus meant by calling His disciples His mother, brothers and sisters?

Those who love and follow God through Jesus Christ come into a family relationship with Him and with each other. Because these relationships are spiritual and eternal—in contrast to our human family relationships, which are biological—our family relationships with other followers of Jesus can be stronger, closer and more long-lasting than our human family ties.

Summary: Following Jesus is about a change of heart and belief, but it is often seen as a change of allegiance to the community, bringing dishonour to the extended family, even though this is certainly not intended. The almighty, perfect God is greater than our families and has loved us so much that He was willing to suffer and die to save us. Such love is greater than any human love and demands a greater response. Through Jesus, God calls us into a new family relationship with God and His people.

Topic 16: Would I have to leave my family and culture to follow Jesus?

(First read Question 16 and the answer in the booklet.)

There is often a concern among Asian seekers that following Christ would mean turning their back on their family, culture and religion by "becoming a Christian". Sadly, many families do reject members who leave their faith to follow Jesus, but it is always best for new followers of Jesus to try to maintain as much contact as possible with the family, as the opposition quite often subsides after a while. There is always more opposition for Muslims leaving Islam. Remember that under Islamic *Sharia* law, the penalty for leaving Islam is death, and such people may have to move away from their family for their own physical safety. It is, of course, possible to follow Jesus within the Asian culture and there are many Asian Christians who do. We should make every effort to help new believers to remain within their culture, and not impose on them cultural changes.

4. What aspects of your family life and culture would be compatible with following Jesus?

This question aims to show that most things in family life, customs and culture (such as what we eat and wear) are still compatible with following Jesus. This should reassure people that they would not have to give up all their heritage and culture to follow Christ.

5. Are there any cultural practices or family customs that you think would be incompatible with following Jesus?

Worship of other gods and certain religious customs will, however, not be compatible with being a follower of Jesus. Attending religious places for social events such as weddings or funerals will still be fine, and there is nothing wrong with eating food offered to idols or wearing certain items of dress, as long as we understand that they do not mean anything spiritually (see 1 Corinthians 8 v 4-8 and Romans 14). Who we marry will be a big issue as followers of Jesus should only marry those who also follow Him. This is an important topic and you will find a much more detailed discussion in the book *Notes for the Journey* (see page 118).

6. How does God view family and culture?

These passages will briefly explore teaching concerning our responsibilities towards our families, and the flexibility of the Christian faith with regard to cultural customs.

Read Exodus 20 v 12

Explain that this is one of the Ten Commandments—the main laws that God gave to His people through Moses over 3,000 years ago. This commandment shows that respect for parents is one of God's priorities.

a. What do you think it means to honour your father and mother?

Honouring our fathers and mothers must mean to show them love, obedience and respect but not necessarily to obey everything they say. If they were to tell us to do something wrong, we would need respectfully to decline. (For example, if our parents were criminals, we should not join with them in stealing.)

Read 1 Corinthians 9 v 19-23

Explain that the law mentioned in these verses is the Law of Moses, which commanded many food restrictions, customs of ritual cleansing, clothing and festival days, etc.

b. What is God's attitude to cultural customs?

We can adapt to fit in with different customs according to the relevant culture, and indeed we should do so in order to relate to those from different cultural backgrounds. Examples of this might include Christian worship with Asian music, choosing to have an arranged marriage (for those who wish it—certainly not being forced into marriage), wearing Asian clothes, or eating the same food as before. The closeness of Asian extended family relationships can be maintained and widened out to the whole church fellowship.

c. What is your conclusion about what would have to change if you follow Jesus? Would you have to leave your family and culture?

Your heart would need to change but your love and respect for your family and most of your cultural customs should remain or be adapted.

Summary: God wants us to continue to love and respect our families if we follow Jesus, and most cultural customs will be compatible with following Him, except for things that involve the worship of other gods or disobeying direct biblical commands.

You will find more suggestions for follow-up in Part C.

Going further

Leading an Asian person to Christ and follow-up

The whole aim of the booklet and discussion course has been to introduce Asian friends to Jesus and what it means to follow Him. This section will give you some brief ideas on how to lead an Asian person to put their faith in Jesus, and how to nurture and disciple them afterwards.

Leading an Asian person to Christ

Traditional Asian culture has a strong tendency to want to please an honoured friend or teacher. When this is combined with the belief that all religions are valid ways to approach God, then it can result in people from these religious and cultural backgrounds readily agreeing to pray to "commit their lives to Jesus". This may be simply out of a desire to please or not appear rude. They may view a prayer to Jesus as just another way to get spiritual blessing, alongside that offered by other gods and *gurus*, and may think that the more supernatural help they can get, the better. Clearly we have to be careful to try to avoid such a situation.

We need to explain the concept of repentance (without using the word itself, which most would not understand). Repentance means a change of heart or mind, which can be explained as a turning away from our previous beliefs and way of life to follow Jesus. It needs to be emphasised that if we are to commit ourselves to following Jesus, we must leave behind all other gods, *gurus* or religious authorities, and make Him the Lord and Master of our lives. Muslims usually understand that choosing to follow Jesus means leaving Islam.

We also need to explain what faith is, as it is often misunderstood as simple intellectual agreement or belief in the facts about Jesus. To put faith in Jesus is to trust Him as the Lord of our lives to save us from our sins and lead us by His Spirit for the rest of our lives. If a doctor said that we needed an operation, he would ask us to sign a form to give our permission. Once we sign, we have given that doctor the power to do whatever he needs to do, and now our life is in his hands. Jesus asks us to sign our lives over to Him, to save and bless us for ever.

God also promises to give the Holy Spirit to all those who put their trust in Jesus, so that we can live a new life through trusting in His power at work within us to change us. The Holy Spirit of God comes to live in our hearts, to give us the power to stop doing the things we do wrong, and start to grow in living a good life according to God's ways. He wants to make us more and more like Jesus! It is also worth reminding our friend that following Jesus will not necessarily be easy, and there may be much opposition, but God will help us through it all.

Once we have explained all these things and checked that the person is really ready to give their life to Jesus and does not feel under undue pressure, we may want to take them through the following suggested prayer of commitment:

> *Dear Lord God, I turn away from living life my own way,*
> *from following other paths and from all the wrong things*
> *that I have done.*
> *Forgive me through Jesus' death on the cross on my behalf.*
> *I trust in Him to be my Saviour and Lord.*
> *Jesus, I give you all that I am and have, so that You may be*
> *the Lord and Master of my life for ever by the power of your*
> *Holy Spirit. Amen*

Note: It is not the words of the prayer that save anyone but, rather, the attitude of repentance and faith that they express. Some may think that just repeating the words has some kind of spiritual power to save them. We need to emphasise that faith is the key.

Once someone has put their faith in the Lord Jesus Christ, they have become a member of the family of God—the church—and our brother or sister in Christ. We have a responsibility before God to nurture and care for them, and to stand by them if trouble comes because of their new faith.

Remember that growing in Christ is a lifelong process for all of us and particularly for somebody coming from a different faith background. We need to give people time and space to develop their own walk with God, and not rush them into things that we, as those who have followed Jesus longer, may take for granted.

Particular struggles

Those from a Muslim background may have an ongoing struggle in accepting the deity of Christ; while those from a Hindu, Buddhist or Sikh background may have similar struggles in accepting that He is the *only* way to God. We need to be patient and continue to support our new brothers and sisters through their doubts and questions.

Many, especially those from a Muslim background, will come under extreme pressure from their families and the wider religious community to return to their original faith, as soon as it becomes known that they are now following Jesus. For this reason, it is unwise to encourage such a new believer to proclaim their faith immediately. Pray for the right time; even Jesus did not immediately proclaim Himself as the Messiah at the beginning of His ministry, but waited for God's right time.

For some, this right time may be early in their walk with Christ; while it may be wise to allow others to grow stronger in their new spiritual life before facing opposition and maybe outright persecution. Be aware that, if it becomes publicly known that a Muslim has left Islam, the *Sharia,* or Islamic law, demands that they be put to death. This means that they may never be able to return to their country of origin without putting their life at risk, and they may even be threatened with physical attack. Hindus, Buddhists and Sikhs are not usually in physical danger, but will almost always face the displeasure of their extended family and the wider community.

They will face many challenges at home, with the pressure to follow traditional practices, from worshipping at the family shrine or engaging in ancestor worship, to using charms and ritual practices, and perhaps marriage to a person who does not follow Jesus.

The majority of converts from Asian religious backgrounds take a long time to get the courage to tell their community about their new faith in Jesus, and many never progress beyond being secret believers. It is particularly hard for women as they are more vulnerable to suffering violence, and also for children who are still under the authority of their parents. Sadly, many converts from Asian religious backgrounds fail to grow in their new faith due to these and other pressures.

Baptism and church involvement

In an ideal world, baptism can and should follow as soon as someone is clear about putting their faith in Jesus. It is almost always, however, an extremely sensitive issue with the extended family and community, as it is a public declaration of the person's new faith.

Some families may be happy for their relative to follow Jesus as long as it remains a private faith that is hidden from the community. This highlights the significance of baptism as a physical act of putting faith into action. There is often spiritual and human opposition to this important step of obedience to Christ, and we need to pray and support those who come forward to be baptised. As we have said before, do not push or pressurise in this area, but let the Holy Spirit guide the new believers and those supporting them.

It would be a disgrace if our Asian friend were to lose their family, friends and community through following Jesus and only get church meetings in return! We must become the **real family of God** that Jesus intended, in order to support such new brothers and sisters. They will often feel caught between communities, and they need to know that they are fully accepted in their new identity in the body of Christ. Offering hospitality is very important in Asian culture and younger people often refer to older people as "uncle" or "aunty". Learn as much as you can about their background and culture to find ways of making them feel more at home. Those born or brought up in western countries may find it much easier to adapt.

We should give time for the Holy Spirit to work in their conscience, rather than demand immediate changes that might be plain to us, but can involve major trauma to a new believer and their family and community relationships. Taking down statues and pictures of gods and *gurus* is an obvious step, but it will immediately advertise their change of faith to others. Gently teach and encourage them to do this but let them do it in their own time.

Attendance at religious venues is fine for social obligations, such as marriages and funerals, but encourage them not to take part in worship (see 2 Kings 5 v 17-19). Be careful not to promote unnecessary change which distances them even more from their community. Some over-zealous Christians have insisted that converts from Sikhism remove their turbans and bangles, even though the Lord is concerned with the heart, not outward appearances (see John 7 v 24). One of the greatest Christian preachers that India ever had, Sadhu Sundar Singh, was from a Sikh background and wore the turban and clothes of a traditional Sikh holy man!

As much as possible, introduce them to other followers of Jesus from the same background as this will be an enormous encouragement.

You will find much more on all these topics in *Notes for the Journey,* which explores what it means to follow Jesus as an Asian (see page 118 for details). The book is written for those beginning to follow Jesus, but will also be valuable for you to read and perhaps work through with your friends.

I.D. International Discipleship Course is a similar book covering the same topics, without specific illustrations from South Asian culture (see page 118 for details).

You will find more suggestions for follow-up in the next section on resources.

Resources

Website material and courses for seekers

www.southasianconcern.org
Material about Jesus from a South Asian perspective.

www.lighthouseicc.org.uk
Stories of people who have started to follow Jesus;
how to begin to follow Jesus ("Built on the Rock");
further answers to questions about the Christian faith.

www.alpha.org
Alpha is a series of interactive sessions that freely explore the basics of
the Christian faith.

www.christianityexplored.org
Christianity Explored is based on the Gospel of Mark and so provides
an ideal opportunity to learn more about Jesus, His identity and His
mission.

www.southasianconcern.org/prayer_room/detail/discover
Discover looks at life issues (with particular relevance to Asians) and
the story of the Bible (with focus on the life and teaching of Jesus).

www.friendsinternational.org.uk
The Visa Course is intended for international students (particularly language students), covering the basics of Christian faith in simple language.

www.almassira.org
Al Massira ("The Journey") presents the Christian faith through a chronological overview of the Bible. It centres the Christian faith in its original middle-eastern context and so is particularly suitable for Muslims from that background.

www.aradhnamusic.com
Worship music in a fusion of eastern and western music styles, "centred around spiritual enlightenment and transformation", building bridges between cultures.

Discipleship for new believers from Asian backgrounds

Built on the Rock
Clive Thorne, Southampton Lighthouse International Church

Notes for the Journey: Following Jesus, Staying South Asian
C. Rasiah and Robin Thomson, South Asian Concern, 2011

I.D. International Discipleship Course
Friends International, 2013

Training resources

Friendship First (www.friendshipfirst.org)
An interactive, non-specialist course in six sessions. It enables Christians to approach their Muslim friends with confidence by equipping them with the skill and resources needed to be an effective witness to Jesus Christ.

East+West (www.southasianconcern.org)
A course which helps you understand the cultural and religious background and practices of South Asians, from basics to more advanced guidelines on communicating with people of other faiths. It can be run as a one-day course or a series of shorter events.

Religions

(very basic introductions from the vast number available)

A Christian's Pocket Guide to Buddhism
Alex Smith, Christian Focus Publications, 2009

A Christian's Pocket Guide to Islam
Patrick Sookhdeo, Christian Focus Publications, 2010

A very short introduction to Hinduism
Kim Knott, Oxford University Press, 1998

Lions, Princesses, Gurus: Reaching your Sikh Neighbour
Ram Gidoomal & Margaret Wardell, Highland, 1996

Mohammed
Maxime Rodinson, Pelican, 1974

A few more books

A Christian's Pocket Guide to the Chinese
OMF, Christian Focus Publications, 2008

A Christian's Pocket Guide to the Japanese
OMF, Christian Focus Publications, 2008

Chapatis for Tea: Reaching your Hindu Neighbour
Ram Gidoomal & Margaret Wardell, Highland, 1994

Engaging with Hindus
Robin Thomson, Good Book Company, 2014 (forthcoming)

Grace for Muslims?
Steve Bell, Authentic, 2006

Good News for Asians in Britain
Sally Sutcliffe (ed), Grove Books Ltd, 1998

Hinduism
H.L. Richard, William Carey Library, Pasadena, 1998, 2001

Islam and Christian witness
Martin Goldsmith, Authentic, 1991

Looking for Directions: towards an Asian spirituality
Sonal Davda, Suneel Shivdasani, Robin Thomson & Margaret Wardell, South Asian Concern, 2006

Walking the Way of the Cross with our Hindu Friends
Ellen Alexander & Robin Thomson (eds), Interserve, Bangalore, 2011. With accompanying DVD.

Stories

Coming to Britain: An Immigrant's story (DVD)
CTA, distributed by Trinity Vision

Death of a Guru
Rabi Maharaj with Dave Hunt, Hodder & Stoughton, 1978

I dared to call him Father
Bilquis Sheikh, Baker, 1978, 2000

Light out of darkness
Clive Thorne, Southampton Lighthouse International Church

Persian Springs
Pauline Selby, Highland Books, 2001

Sindhi Journeys of Faith
D and C Mahtani, May 2010

Resource organisations

Friends International
Building friendships with international students in the UK
www.friendsinternational.org.uk

International Students, Inc
Sharing Christ's love with international students
www.isionline.org

Interserve
Following Christ among the peoples of Asia and the Middle East
www.interserve.org

Japan Christian Link
Educating, encouraging and equipping Christians so that the good news of Jesus Christ will be proclaimed clearly among Japanese people.
www.jclglobal.org

Kitab
Provider of books, literature, DVDs and videos in more than 35 languages to help serve Christians in their outreach to people of other faiths. **www.kitab.org.uk**

MGL Multilingual
Books, music, DVD and other resources in most Asian languages.
www.multilingual-southasian.com

OMF International
Serves the church and bring the gospel to many of the countries in East Asia. **www.omf.org**

South Asian Concern
Equipping the church to share the good news of Jesus with South Asians around the world. **www.southasianconcern.org**

South Asian Forum of the Evangelical Alliance
A forum for South Asian Christians in the UK to encourage, support and equip each other for mission, and to represent their concerns to Government, media and the wider Church. **www.saf.eauk.org**

Southampton Lighthouse International Church
Sharing the good news of the Lord Jesus Christ with people of all backgrounds. **www.lighthouseicc.org.uk**

The Good Book Company
International publisher and resource distributor.
www.thegoodbook.co.uk (UK); www.thegoodbook.com (USA); www.thegoodbook.com.au (Australia); www.thegoodbook.co.nz (New Zealand)

Discovering Jesus course office
www.discovering-jesus.com
Tel (UK): 020 7520 3831. Tel: (int): +44 207 520 3831
email: info@discovering-jesus.com

Notes

Notes

Notes

*Chr*istianity
E✗PLORED
One life. What's it all about?

Christianity Explored is a relaxed and informal way of introducing people to Jesus and is also great for anyone wanting to brush up on the basics of the Christian faith.

The structure of each evening is simple: an informal meal or snack, a short Bible Study, a talk (either live or from the DVD) and a discussion based on the talk.

It gives people time and space to think about the big questions of life and to explore the person at the heart of the Christian faith – Jesus Christ.

How does the course work?

Over 7 weeks, you will journey through the Gospel of Mark exploring the identity, mission and call of Jesus – who he is, why he came and what it means to follow him. There is plenty of time to ask questions and discuss the claims of Jesus and their implications for our lives.

Training leaders

As well as faithfully presenting the gospel, *Christianity Explored* equips leaders to share their faith and answer difficult questions from the lips of Jesus. The leader's guide contains a wealth of training material designed to inspire, encourage and inform course leaders in their evangelism.

Find out more at www.christianityexplored.org/course

What do I need to run the course?

Leader's Guide

Contains everything you need to lead a course and works alongside the Handbook and DVD. Features comprehensive training material and advice.

Handbook

Easy-to-use format contains everything a guest needs for the course as well as a section on the reliability of Mark's Gospel.

DVD

This beautifully shot, award-winning DVD presented by Rico Tice works alongside the Handbook and Leader's Guide. It includes English subtitles for the hard of hearing and subtitles in 14 other languages, including Spanish. It is even available in electronic format to download by episode if you want to display it on a computer.

Want to run CE in a different language?
See what's available at:
www.thegoodbook.co.uk/cetranslations

thegoodbook
C O M P A N Y

Opening up the Bible

At The Good Book Company, we are dedicated to helping Christians and local churches grow. We believe that God's growth process always starts with hearing clearly what He has said to us through His timeless word—the Bible.

Ever since we opened our doors in 1991, we have been striving to produce resources that honour God in the way the Bible is used. We have grown to become an international provider of user-friendly resources to the Christian community, with believers of all backgrounds and denominations using our Bible studies, books, evangelistic resources, DVD-based courses and training events.

We want to equip ordinary Christians to live for Christ day by day, and churches to grow in their knowledge of God, their love for one another, and the effectiveness of their outreach.

Call us for a discussion of your needs or visit one of our local websites for more information on the resources and services we provide.

UK & Europe: www.thegoodbook.co.uk
North America: www.thegoodbook.com
Australia: www.thegoodbook.com.au
New Zealand: www.thegoodbook.co.nz

UK & Europe: 0333 123 0880
North America: 866 244 2165
Australia: (02) 6100 4211
New Zealand (+64) 3 343 1990

www.christianityexplored.org

Our partner site is a great place for those exploring the Christian faith, with a clear explanation of the good news, powerful testimonies and answers to difficult questions.

One life.
What's it all about?